COME & TAKE IT!

The Story of the

Tumlinson Family

Hon. Eric Dick, Esq.

Dedication

To my daughters Grace and Caroline, I write this book written for you. Please remember the importance of family and the sorrows that we have overcome.

Don't give up.

Don't sell out.

Don't be afraid.

Don't stop growing.

Don't stop learning.

Every day of life is a blessing.

Be the best person you can be.

–Dad

Forward

As a young boy, my grandmother often told exciting tales of the early days of Texas. To this day, I recall the fear in her eyes when discussing the early settler's dealings with Native Americans. These stories and their many lessons were undoubtedly passed down to her in the same manner from her grandparents.

Being a direct descendent of James Tumlinson, my grandmother had much to tell. I recognize that all of her teachings were based on the two fundamental pillars of faith and family that first began with the early Tumlinson settlers. Their faith was a confidence that a higher power guides us all to a greater meaning. The purpose is one of which we always aren't capable of understanding.

For American pioneers, the family was a sacred establishment and, all too often, the very backbone of existence. It was apparent to anyone who knew my grandmother that this notion of the family remained in our lineage. She instilled in those around her the same unconditional love and regard.

It's also worth noting that my grandmother and many of my ancestors came from modest means. That is, there is nearly an unlimited list of things they could not provide. Still, most importantly, my grandmother and her parents before her deeply loved their children, parents, siblings, and relatives. There is a beautiful simplicity to this lifestyle and the meaning behind it. My grandmother and the Tumlinsons settlers were grounded in the belief that all you have in life is your family.

In that respect, it never mattered how much wealth they lacked because their story is full of deep appreciation of what they had. The pillars of faith and family gracefully describe what joined the Tumlinson's together and gave them strength.

Please note that although Texas history is profoundly intertwined with the Tumlinson family, you read very little about them in most history books. A likely reason being that the Tumlinson's thought very little about fame or glory. Instead, they loved their family and held a sincere faith in God. Those two characteristics were more than enough in their minds.

However, when someone interferes with these pillars, they experience a different side of the Tumlinson's. Their sincere love for God and family tied closely to their inclination to fight for these principles. This book is also filled with stories that showcase their tenacity and fearlessness.

A more recent first-hand story was told to me that flickers of the Tumlinson family's tenacity. Edith May, my grandmother's daughter, and my aunt, graduated high school at age fifteen. In 1941, she attended Rice University, often being the only woman in her classes. She graduated in 1944 with a degree in physics.

Unfortunately, her father didn't appreciate the tenacity of the Tumlinson blood that ran through her veins. Indeed, he vehemently opposed it. He held that Edith's college education was a waste of money and that she was only going to school to find a husband. When Edith asked her father for financial help, he disapproved.

Determined and fearless, Edith worked many part-time jobs to pay for her college and boarding at the mere age of fifteen. Eventually, she earned enough that she decided to pay her father back for what she calculated he spent raising her. To Edith (and any Tumlinson), that was a grave insult.

Over the years, she did many amazing things, like working at NASA and even writing an episode for The Twilight Zone. Sadly, being a woman, she was forced to use a pseudonym. In the end, despite all her success, the two most important assets to her were still the same as her mother's and the same as the early Tumlinson's - faith and family.

Acknowledgment

Danielle, my amazing wife, must be recognized for her works in this book. She was as important to its completion as I was. An indispensable editor, collaborator, and partner, I cannot thank her enough. This book was more brutal to write than I anticipated, yet more satisfying than I could ever have expected. None of this would have been possible without her help. Thank you very much, my love. This book is very much your book as it is mine.

Introduction

Brothers John and James Tumlinson left Arkansas and came to Texas at precisely the right time for them and their families to play significant roles in a historical drama about to unfold. Over the next 25 years, through determined American colonization, the untamed Texas landscape became a civilization of, particularly stubborn-minded independence.

The unsteady hand of the Mexican government, which was, itself, in turmoil, could not contain that feeling. At first, through words, Texas struggled with increasingly violent rebellion and retribution to gain independence from Mexico and become a part of the United States.

The Tumlinsons did not go to Texas to become heroes, leaders, or soldiers. They went as frontiersmen planning to be ranchers and farmers in a land of new opportunities. When they arrived, circumstances were unexpectedly dangerous and uncertain. The Tumlinsons did what pioneering people have always done when pressed: what was necessary.

Much of the information presented herein about the Tumlinson family comes from two books written by descendants of John Jackson Tumlinson Sr.:

1. *Tumlinson, a Genealogy,* published in 1989 by Samuel H. Tumlinson; and
2. *From Whence We Came: John Jackson Tumlinson and Elizabeth Plemmons, Their Descendants, and Connections,* published in 1999 by Verner Lee Bell.

As Samuel laments, the Tumlinsons weren't given to recording their lives. They went about the business of forging the state of Texas and protecting the people who lived there not for glory but for the sake of those who depended on them. Their contributions are recorded in land titles, deeds, military records, the logbooks of Texas Ranger commanders, and stories passed down for generations. What the Tumlinsons, themselves, may have thought or felt, we can only guess by determining their actions.

The Tumlinsons whose actions will be a part of our story are as follows:

John Jackson Tumlinson, Sr.* and his sons:	James Tumlinson (brother of John Jackson Sr.) and his sons:
Thomas Carney Tumlinson	Littleton F. Tumlinson
Peter Tumlinson	James Tumlinson
John Jackson Tumlinson, Jr.	David Carney Tumlinson
Andrew Tumlinson	George W. Tumlinson
Joseph Tumlinson	John Tumlinson

* Please note that both John Sr. and James had other children, many of whom died in childhood. To avoid unnecessary confusion, we will only discuss those who survived to adulthood to participate in the events during the formative years of independent Texas and the Texas Rangers.

It would be simple enough to list the many actions and adventures of the Tumlinsons: they were instrumental in forming the Texas Rangers. They participated in several key battles and incidents in Texas's rebellion against Mexico. Hardly any critical event happened in Texas during the two decades from 1820 to 1840 in which a Tumlinson man was not at least peripherally involved.

However, such a list would be meaningless without understanding the circumstances under which these men found themselves. Caught between two different revolutions, under possible siege at any moment by Natives or Mexican armies, and ruled, only loosely, by a government in constant change. Confused by its newfound independence, Mexico suffered two outright coups in its first 15 years of existence. And, after a legal election voted them out, Mexican Federalists refused to relinquish control. The irony is that legal elections were a point for which the Federalists, themselves, had fought.

Meanwhile, the residents of Texas, Mexicans, and Anglo settlers alike were on their own when it came to the necessities of safety and representation but subject to the Mexican government when it came to taxes and laws.

Presiding at first in the background of Mexican politics and then coming to the forefront through impressively calculated manipulation, the Mexican President and General Santa Anna – supposedly a friend to the Anglo settlers of Texas – would eventually push the issue to the point of all-out war.

So, this, too, is a story of the Mexican Revolution, the migration of Americans to Texas, the formation of the

Texas Rangers, the stirrings of rebellion against a neglectful government, the push back against the terror of the Comanche tribe, and the battle for Texan independence. Scratch the surface of any one of these historical events, and you'll find a Tumlinson son nearby, doing what needed to be done.

Table of Contents

CHAPTER ONE: ONWARD TO TEXAS

The Godforsaken Land..16

The Lead King Makes a Deal 21

A Young Lawyer from New Orleans 23

A Family from North Carolina....................................25

Alone in the Wilderness 17

The Native Threat...36

Alcalde 33

CHAPTER TWO: THE TEXAS RANGERS

Any Man with a Gun...38

Rangers...40

The First Ranger to Die 43

Stephen Austin Returns 45

Santa Anna 47

The Mexican Empire 49

The Death of Thomas Carney Tumlinson 49

1824: The Republic of Mexico 51

No More Easy Pickings 54

CHAPTER THREE: FEARS OF MEXICO

Visitors from Mexico City 58

Napoleon of the West 58

On the Brazos and Colorado Rivers 60

Peter Tumlinson Returns to Texas 68

Santa Anna's Next Move 69

War Dogs 70

Presidios in Texas 72

Two Conventions 75

The Trials of Stephen Austin 78

Farías at the Helm 81

Santa Anna Switches Sides 82

CHAPTER FOUR: COME AND TAKE IT

1835 84

Officially Texas Rangers 86

More Trouble in Anahuac 86

A Changed Man 87

Come and Take It 87

Provisional Government 94

Volunteer Army of the People of Texas 96

The Fate of the Cannon 102

The Provisional Government Crumbles 104

A Daring Rescue 107

CHAPTER FOUR: BLOODY REVOLUTION

Santa Anna Comes to Texas 112

Texas Rangers Come When Called 116

No Reinforcements from the Provisional Government 116

The Fall – and Fallout – of the Alamo 123

Runaway Scrape..126

The Battle of Coleto Creek 126

The Goliad Massacre 130

A Long Road to San Jacinto..131

Battle of San Jacinto 134

The Capture of the Great Santa Anna................................136

The Tumlinson Family in the Texas Revolution..................138

End of the Texas Revolution...139

The Spirit of Texas 140

Horse Marines: A Texas Rangers Story 142

CHAPTER SIX: COMANCHE WAR

Threat from the North 145

Penniless..146

President Sam Houston..150

Jilted 150

Austin 153

President Lamar and Comanche Aggression......................154

One More Try for a Treaty 157

The Council House Fight...158

Comanche Vengeance 161

The Battle of Plum Creek...164

A Revolver to the Rescue 167

CHAPTER SEVEN: THE PROUD STATE OF TEXAS

Annexation at Last...170

Texas Moves On, and the Rangers Come Along 173

The Tumlinson Brothers' Fates..173

Texas Legends 180

Chapter One:

Onward to Texas

The Godforsaken Land

The Sabine River became the border between the United States and Spanish Texas in 1819. The river is the gentle inward curve of Louisiana's far western edge. The Sabine was only one of several rivers to follow long arms downward toward the Gulf of Mexico through the vast territory of Spanish Texas. A brave traveler making his way southwest would next encounter the rivers Neches, Trinity, Brazos, Colorado, Guadalupe, San Antonio, and Nueces. Finally, should he survive the trip all the way south, he would cross the Rio Grande – but of course, survival couldn't be guaranteed.

If it was not godforsaken, the land remained relatively well forsaken by almost everyone else. Stepping into the endless spread of land west of the Sabine or north of the Rio Grande would put one in the wild, virtually unknown country – a territory so remote, so far north from Mexico City that the Spanish monarchy chose to ignore it mostly.

There were so few Spanish-Mexican citizens living there that the government was all but nonexistent. Terrifying tribes of Natives besieged the land, the likes of whom the Spanish had no desire to engage. The most fearsome of all had emerged almost ironically: during the hundreds of years that Spain held this land, a generally quiet and unassuming native tribe called the Comanche had discovered, then mastered, horsemanship – with horses brought to the ground by the Spanish themselves – to become an enemy of legendary ferocity.

For over 300 years, the various Native tribes had used the territory as hunting grounds but had made few attempts to cultivate it in any other way; as the United States spread westward, more and more Native groups migrated into the relatively ungoverned region of Texas. They were, over that period, in frequent conflict with the Mexican residents of Texas, so few as to be considered a minor threat to the Native population.

Yet, while Spain chose to have little to do with Spanish Texas, those stubborn pioneers from the other side of the Sabine most determinedly continued to cross that river, with or without permission. Americans seemed unable to quench their desire to move ever further into the unknown, where they risked their very lives to stake out a patch of land and see what could be accomplished. No terror, weather, disease, nor hardship seemed able to stop them.

The Spanish government had little time to worry about these illegal immigrants, who would likely not die without having caused too much trouble. Mexico was the more pressing problem. The Spanish colony of Mexico had been fighting for its independence for the past decade. A tenth of the Mexican population died in the war, and still, they fought. They were rampantly illiterate, desperately poor, stricken often by famine or smallpox, and suffering a shocking infant mortality rate. Still, they fought for independence from the only government they had ever known.

At last, Spain relinquished control in 1821, leaving Mexico reeling in its absence. The newly independent country had little idea of how to govern a republic, so accustomed to monarchy. Indeed, they initially operated as an empire with Emperor Iturbide at its head. Only in 1824 would Mexico, at last, declare itself a republic and form a tenuous constitution, though this would not end their troubles. Over the next decade, the government established in Mexico City changed leadership multiple times as they felt their way toward a version of democracy.

But this, again, left that vast and lonely territory between the Sabine and the Rio Grande largely ignored and underpopulated. A scant number of Tejanos (Mexican Texans) peopled Texas, the most remote of all the Mexican states. The toughened Tejanos scratched together a mysterious, difficult living throughout the harsh terrain, unpredictable weather, and Native threat. However, their presence alone was at least an initial deterrent to Native attack.

Regardless, Mexico could not convince its citizens to relocate to this place. History and common sense tell the truth: unpopulated land is an untamed land. Someone must go and live there and shed the blood and sweat required.

The Mexicans turned to those who were already making themselves at home: settlers from the United States. Whereas Mexicans wouldn't go to Texas, the American pioneers continued to slip over the Sabine and push onward. And while the American pioneers considered the Mexican Tejanos to be a buffer between themselves and the Native Tribes, the Tejanos looked at the American pioneers precisely.

The world had suffered a hard-hitting economic crisis in the Panic of 1819, and the United States was no exception to the fallout. Those who were already poor were somehow hit the hardest, and both frontiersmen, with dwindling resources and city-dwellers, left unemployed and desperate, looked hopefully for a fresh start. Soon, there would come an opportunity of previously unimagined generosity, and all one had to do was offer up his life in the gamble.

The Lead King Makes a Deal

Moses Austin was a man who knew how to make a fortune but not how to keep one. Austin was born in Connecticut in 1761. Twice in his busy life, he made himself a rich man, first lead mining in Virginia, where he gained national recognition as the "Lead King."

The Lead King, however, couldn't keep himself out of debt. He lost everything, left the problems to his brother, and fled to Spanish Louisiana (now Missouri).

In Louisiana, Austin became a Spanish citizen, and Spain granted him a league of land. Part of his promise to Spain was to bring more colonists to the area. Here, Austin founded the first American settlement west of the Mississippi River, the town of Potosi, which still exists, with a modest population of around 2,000 people. The voluminous lead deposits in the area and Austin's own experience in mining allowed him to rebuild his empire.

The Panic of 1819 also affected Moses Austin, who had most of his money invested in banking, wiping out his second fortune. Never one to rest or settle, Austin decided to propose a new colonial endeavor in Spanish Texas. He traveled to San Antonio de Bexar, the current seat of the Texas government, to meet with the Spanish governor of Texas, Antonio Maria Martinez. Austin crossed many of those Texan rivers to go deep into the lonely territory, and there to the governor proposed the movement of American settlers to Texas. Governor Martinez gave Moses Austin a land grant and permission to settle 300 families in Texas.

Moses Austin would never have the chance, however. On his return trip to Missouri, he contracted pneumonia. By the time he reached Missouri, the Lead King was so ill that he could barely arrange for the bequeathing of the land grant to his son, Stephen Fuller Austin, before passing away in 1821.

A Young Lawyer from New Orleans

At age 24, Stephen Austin practiced law in New Orleans. He received a letter from his mother relaying two pieces of shocking news: first that his father had died. Second, his father's legacy left young Austin in charge of an incredible deal in Mexican Texas – some madness about bringing colonists to the wild area and settling them there.

Ever the responsible son, Austin rode out for San Antonio de Bexar to investigate the claim's validity. During his journey to the city, Austin learned that Mexico had gained its independence from Spain after ten years of fighting. This completely changed the circumstances of the arrangements Moses Austin made. Would the new Mexican government even acknowledge the deal?

Austin was a far more level-headed intellectual than the average adventuring pioneer, however, and had a way of impressing officials. Governor Martinez, the governor who had granted land to Austin's father, reaffirmed the deal with Stephen Austin and further permitted him to explore between Bexar and the Brazos River to find the most suitable location for his colony. It was by no means the last time Austin would have to renegotiate and reconfirm his land grant in the confusion that followed for about three years after Mexico achieved independence. Still, he was consistently able to obtain agreement to more or less the same terms. Even Emperor Iturbide, during his short reign, confirmed Austin's grant.

The authorities at first permitted Austin to bring 300 families to his colony – famously referred to as the "Old 300". While he might have initially been uncertain about his father's impulsive deal, the younger Austin's explorations of the area convinced him that Texas was, indeed, a land of great and worthwhile potential for his interests. His philosophy of "conquering" was never one of carving a path through conflict. He was not interested in warfare. Austin would consistently remain a voice of reason throughout the years to come, believing that settlement could best be achieved with hard work in developing the land into functioning farms, ranches, and industries of mining and woodcutting. For many years, he remained a champion of peace until the time came when circumstances forced him to change his mind.

But these were early days still. Upon his return to New Orleans, Austin advertised the availability of inexpensive land along the Brazos and Colorado Rivers, now available to American settlers – provided they were willing to become Mexican citizens and convert to Catholicism, at least on paper. Stephen Austin was not the only American frontiersman/entrepreneur to make such a deal with the Mexican government, either – others, such as Sterling C. Robertson, Green DeWitt, and Benjamin R. Milam, had land grants for colonies of a hundred or more families to return to the same general area, and would each play parts in the events to come.

The economic crisis of 1819 still held a stranglehold throughout the United States, and no lack of volunteers stood ready to take advantage of the idea of a fresh start in a new land. Austin returned with settlers accompanying him or following closely behind, and among these were John Jackson Tumlinson, Jr. and James Tumlinson and their families.

A Family from North Carolina

In 1822, John Jackson Tumlinson Sr. (born 1776) brought his wife, Elizabeth Plemmons Tumlinson, and their children to the Colorado District of the Mexican territory of Texas.

They were one of 300 families, most of whom arrived by 1825, to join the colonists gathered there between the Colorado and Brazos Rivers by empresario Stephen F. Austin. Austin had inherited a "deal" from his father at almost precisely the wrong time to bring colonists to an underpopulated and wild territory that was about to undergo a complete change in authority.

Strangely, however, the dealings of the government in Mexico City, or even the local Mexican authority in San Antonio de Felipe, seldom had much control over the American colonists who arrived in this new wild landscape. Whatever Spain or Mexico's intentions were to populate the area, the Americans brought America along with them and would change the course of history where they staked their claims.

The Tumlinsons began their journey in North Carolina, where John Sr. was born. A long journey westward across the young United States took them from North Carolina to Tennessee, Illinois, and Arkansas, pausing for months or years at a time in each state as their children were born – and sometimes, sadly, died.

They remained for many years in the established community of Tumlinson Township in Crawford County, Arkansas. Even after John Sr. and Elizabeth Tumlinson eventually moved on, Tumlinson Township remained home to many members of their extended family, including siblings of John and James and the descendants of those siblings, and children of the couples who had grown old enough to settle down with their own families and wished to go no further south. The little knot of close families eventually absorbed into the larger townships of Crawford County.

Still, the township might have remained John Sr. and Elizabeth's home for good, were it not for the two separate but complementary happenings. First, the United States Government considered giving the land on which the Tumlinson Township had settled to Natives as a reserve, despite protestations from the colonists. They had so improved the ground that it was by rights theirs. Second, a timely siren's song crossed the Sabine River from Mexican Texas into Louisiana and New Orleans, where the news spread fast. A fantastic prospect became available for stouthearted adventurers.

That prospect was the abundant land of Texas: there lay the promise of fertile tracts of loamy farmland and grazing lands so vast that one might not see from one side to the other with the naked eye, given away for a pittance to any American pioneer sturdy enough to make the journey. Rumors circulated, some whispered and some brandished boldly, of land like the Garden of Eden with abundant game, a pleasant climate, and trees that had fruit fairly dripping off them.

Following the trail of those who had arrived before him, John Sr. established his headright on the Colorado River near Beason's Ferry (the area now Columbus, Texas). He, Elizabeth, and their seven children made their home alongside other settlers like themselves, such as the Beasons, Kuykendalls, Morrisons, and Gillelands.

John Tumlinson Sr.'s brother, James Tumlinson (born 1781 and married to a woman named Elizabeth), came with his family and accompanied his older brother to settle in the Colorado region with his many children. The colony of pioneers, well managed as it was by their empresario Stephen Fuller Austin, kept from starving and establishing something like a society.

Those of Anglo descent who came to settle in Texas was called by several attempted denotations: Texicans, Texasians, Texonians, even Texilingans. They called themselves the Texians.

These first Texian settlers found themselves not in the Garden of Eden but an unpredictable purgatory. Spain and Mexico wanted immigrants, and for a time, it was a seller's market. The seductive stories of the bounties awaiting brave souls in Texas had neglected to mention the heat, the wildlife (some large enough to kill humans, some small enough to transmit malaria), or the multiple Native tribes who already claimed this place as their home and hunting grounds. The Tumlinsons came to a place where law, safety, and survival were left in their own hands.

Alone in the Wilderness

Not long after he brought his first settlers to the Colorado District, doubts about the Mexican government forced Stephen Austin to return to Mexico City to renegotiate the terms of his colonization arrangement. Other versions of the tumultuous Mexican government had made the original arrangement and the transfer to Stephen Austin from Moses Austin. Austin technically went of his own volition, but in truth, he had little choice if he wanted to ensure that the structure of his colonization deal remained the same.

As was the case with many aspects of settling in Texas, the timing was almost perfectly wrong. With no choice but to make his pleas directly to the government's wishes, Austin left the colonists without leadership in circumstances for which none of them were truly prepared.

The conditions along the Brazos were far more dangerous than anyone had expected, with heat, snakes, alligators, disease, unexpected shortages of supplies, and the threat of hostile Natives in the surrounding countryside, and no support from the local government. These settlers did not even know if the Mexican Empire (as it briefly was) would grant the land promised to them. By and large, these settlers could not speak the country's language to which they now sought citizenship.

Some families elected to return north; those that remained might have eventually followed, were it not for the appearance of Baron de Bastrop, who assured them that not only would the Imperial Government protect them, but also that they would most certainly receive their titles.

Baron de Bastrop (a pseudonym adopted by Frenchman Felipe Enrique Neri to promote the idea that he was of noble descent – though he was not) was something of an enigmatic, flamboyant ringmaster from the era of Texan colonization. Bastrop was a successful colonizer of the Bexar area himself, an experienced diplomat, well-liked by necessary people. He had befriended Moses Austin and was key in arranging the elder Austin's deal with the Spanish government. He was no less friendly and helpful to Stephen Austin, and, at the time, he was as respected an authority figure as the colonists could hope for in the younger Austin's absence. At any rate, Bastrop encouraged the colonists to elect their officers and get on with the business of living until Austin would, inevitably, return to them in triumph.

The Native Threat

The Native tribes of Texas were many, Cherokee, Lipan Apaches, Tawakonis, Wacos, Tonkawas, Delawares,

Karankawas, and Caddos. Some tribes were indigenous; some were forced into the area by the westward expansion of the United States. Native relationships with the Tejanos (Mexican Texans) and the Texians varied from standoffishness to looting and harassment to outright hostility. However, some trade and temporary neighboring did occur, especially if the Natives had been "Christianized" by the Spanish missions in the area. Some Natives, and it seemed the Karankawas in particular, quickly deduced that these new settlers were easy prey who had many items worth taking – and they took advantage of this situation.

On the whole, Texas belonged to the Native tribes, but the viewpoint of those colonizing the area, from the Mexican government to the colonists themselves, was that the land "belonged" to whoever's name was on the deed. Of course, looking with hindsight changes the dynamic of what unfolded. We must, at this point, view the events through the eyes of those who came to live on Texas land. We know with certainty that both sides of the fight suffered unspeakable losses.

The sheer terror of the Comanche tribe was the most significant threat Texians felt. The Comanche was ruthlessly effective in their raids. Help could neither be summoned nor organized before a raiding Comanche party struck and was gone again. Their braves were so gifted in horsemanship that they seemed supernatural. The Comanche empire claimed a massive swath of land north of the newly settled colonies called the Comancheria, which included a significant chunk of Texas and portions of Colorado, Kansas, New Mexico, and Oklahoma.

One of the significant reasons Spain and Mexico encouraged European settlement in Texas was to create a buffer between Mexico and the Comancheria. Imagine the surprise of the colonists to learn that their invitation to this land of plenty included their use as human shields.

Alcalde

The Americans who first settled in Texas to become Texians learned that they had no courts, police, or institutions of any kind. The local Mexican government, meager as it was, was unable or unwilling to provide anything in the way of help. Mob rule decided most cases where "justice" was required.

But the people of the Colorado District did appoint officials. Texians followed a man who had proven his worth "under fire," and John Jackson Tumlinson, Sr., had already proven his worth by arriving in Texas with his family and establishing his headright successfully ahead of most other settlers.

At Baron de Bastrop's suggestion that the colonists choose their leaders, they elected Tumlinson as the *alcalde* of the Colorado district of Austin's territory. An alcalde functioned as a sort of combined mayor, sheriff, and justice of the peace, taking care of the colonists' domestic troubles and needs in his jurisdiction.

For example, early Texas settler Noah Smithwick, whose account of his experiences in the days of the Old 300 makes a most amusing read, recounts in his book *The Evolution of a State*, attending a wedding alcalde officiated in the "American" style. The bride and groom had to sign a contract to avail themselves of a priest's services as soon as possible – for you will recall that the settlers had all technically converted to Catholicism when they accepted their land grants. Whether they actually did so or just took the alcalde's authority to wed them is uncertain.

Another settler of the Old 300 families, Robert Kuykendall, was an Arkansas fur trader who had arrived simultaneously with the Tumlinson family. Kuykendall had some peacekeeping experience of his own. However, what he had been doing was kindly called vigilantism and might have involved more than a few instances of murder – but terms were flexible in the wildland of Texas. Along with a veteran American soldier named Moses Morrison, Kuykendall was given charge of the "military" of the Colorado District.

No one can envy the task given to these men: the care and protection of a colony that was, at any moment, on the brink of destruction and which had not the supplies nor the organization to defend its interests. One of the first duties Tumlinson carried out was the investigation of a double murder, wherein it appeared four Spaniards had murdered a homesteader and an American tradesman. This resulted in the arrest of two Spanish army deserters.

Lawlessness was pretty rampant, and while Natives were the most intimidating and obvious threat, piracy and murderous banditry thrived from other quarters in the untamed landscape. The size of the area and the lack of authority saw violence running rampant in Colorado and

Brazos Districts. Alcalde Tumlinson had an idea for increasing the protection of the colonists.

Chapter Two:

The Texas Rangers

Any Man with a Gun

In the early days of the Old 300, any man with a gun in Texas was the militia, whether he received the official title or not (there would be no "official title" of a Texas Ranger until 1835). A man (or a woman in the same circumstances) had a family and a homestead to protect. So, with no other law enforcement or militia on his side, he meted out safety and justice himself or died in the process.

Having worked together to protect the Colorado District for about two years, in 1823, Tumlinson and Kuykendall decided that the settlers desperately needed a more optimized form of help, which extended beyond mere reaction to signs of trouble: a force that could subvert trouble before it arrived.

They wrote to the provincial governor, José Félix Trespalacios, to ask his permission to raise a volunteer company of fifteen men. Tumlinson suggested this force protect newly arrived settlers through a series of blockhouses that would start near the mouth of the

Colorado River and utilize the river to transport militiamen by boat.

Governor Trespalacios gave his approval, and so Tumlinson and Kuykendall formed a squad commanded by the U.S. Army veteran Moses Morrison (for whom Tumlinson had great admiration). Morrison's men are generally considered the first iteration of the organization that would become the Texas Rangers in a decade. By May of 1823, their roster of volunteers included nine men, not Morrison and Kuykendall: five farmers, one tailor, and one carpenter. The other two were possibly a currier and a schoolmaster, but the records are uncertain.

Tumlinson and Kuykendall organized the ranging company from the beginning to deal with Native threats. Kuykendall often took their company out to scout incidences of disappeared colonists, traders, or supply shipments and found not only Natives responsible but Mexican outlaws and opportunistic American pioneers (sometimes a combination of these groups). Regardless, Kuykendall's methods of "discouraging" criminals (which included personal touches, like leaving decapitated heads upon spikes) were swift and shocking and quickly discouraged vandalism and theft, at least within Austin's territory. Kuykendall never hesitated to meet out brutal punishments, and the fearsome reputation of the group spread quickly.

Rangers

The occupation of "ranger" finds its roots in the Middle Ages of the British Isles: this was a man one could send into a lawless, unpredictable land, trusting him to scout out and quell trouble by whatever means he saw fit. The mythical ranger retains the romantic ideal of a noble intelligence gatherer, plus a qualified judge, jury, and executioner.

The archetype is a favorite of fiction – isn't even superspy James Bond a sort of ranger who follows missions at his discretion with a license to kill?

In the early 19th century, Texas was so enormous and empty, and the threats of Native attack on settlers were so constant that there was nothing romantic or idealized about its need for ranging. There was no other feasible way to patrol the vast space.

A ranger was not a regular army; a ranger would disdain the trappings of a regular army. They were more independent than that, plus they considered themselves noble volunteers. They were sometimes eccentric and usually brutally effective, or simply brutal, in their methods.

They swooped in when trouble happened and disappeared once it was over. They had no uniforms but usually dressed in tough buckskins; they provided their supplies, and it was said that the only things a Ranger required were a knife, pistol, long rifle (muzzle-loaded, of course), and his horse.

They were accustomed (or learned to be accustomed) to painfully rugged living, sleeping on the ground, going for days or weeks without any of the comforts of home. Therefore the "ranger" role appealed to men who already understood the barren lifestyle: trappers, frontiersmen, and other adventurous types. Although they received no official training and likely very little training of any kind, they fast developed a reputation for being deadeye shots and skilled horsemen. But in truth, any man who had survived in Texas for a certain number of years while protecting his family and homestead had the experience of grabbing a gun and watching his foothold. One did not survive long in Texas without the aid of authoritarian inner resilience, and all citizens had to be ready at a moment's notice to fight.

The Tejanos had already developed their effective system of ranging. Their groups are known colorfully as the "Flying Companies" (Compañías volantes), which patrolled the frontier. These squads of light cavalry responded to Native raiders fast, taking the fight to the Native campsites. They performed extended patrols and had established numerous routes into the Comancheria. Rangers took many lessons from the Flying Companies when it came to tactics. While matters were still friendly between Tejanos and Texians, the Flying Companies and the Rangers often rode together on raids and fought alongside one another.

Many years from their inception, when the political revolution came as Texas attempted to free itself of Mexico, the Rangers seldom had direct involvement. Officials dispatched their groups away from battle areas to assure that there was no Native interference. The Texians had enough to deal with during their revolution without also worrying about raids from native tribes. Therefore, it is essential to remember that the Texas

Rangers and the Texas Revolution were two parallel facets of history, with some men engaging in both.

For our purposes, we will see that men of the Tumlinson family were heavily involved in the heroics of both paths.

The First Ranger to Die

The newly formed ranger company was short on ammunition – while he was away, Austin's colony was short on everything, to be honest. In July of 1823, John Jackson Tumlinson, Sr. and colonist Joseph Newman set out for San Antonio de Bexar to purchase gunpowder and other supplies and negotiate with the local government there to benefit the colonists.

The exact details of Tumlinson's death are uncertain; at least two versions of the story exist with much incomplete information. Tumlinson and Newman encountered a group of Waco Natives, or possibly a combination of Waco and Karankawa Natives, and maybe their Spaniard companion, numbering anywhere from four to thirteen, depending on which version, at the Guadalupe River. Also dependent on the understanding of the tale are the exact events that led to Tumlinson's death. Tumlinson either offered his hand in greeting and was jerked off his horse and killed, or, perceiving a threat, he attacked in self-defense and was killed in response. His body remained forever lost in the river, so the cause of death was undetermined. Mr. Newman, astride a good horse, was able to escape.

When Kuykendall reported Tumlinson's death to the governor, he declared that the colonists would not allow this murder of their alcalde to go unanswered. The effect that John Jackson Tumlinson Sr. 's death had on his sons is apparent. Their grief-stricken anger toward the Native population burned into them a fierce desire to join the organization's ranks that their father had started, the primary function of which was to "deal" with the Native threat. Shortly after John Jackson Sr. 's death, a party of Waco Indians was seen approaching settlements, and these to be the ones assumed to have killed the alcalde.

John Jackson Tumlinson, Jr. raised eleven men, including his younger brother, Joseph Tumlinson (who was only twelve years old at the time), to track the Wacos to their campground. Late at night, as Tumlinson's men neared the suspected party, young Joseph went out as a scout to obtain information on the Wacos' ground and defenses.

When he returned with this information, Tumlinson's group set up and prepared to attack in the morning. The signal for the attack would be a gunshot from John Jackson Tumlinsons Jr. However, Joseph, in his inexperience and anguish, aimed and fired at a Native within his range, a good enough shot to kill the man. The loud report and the Native's dying shout sparked the assault prematurely, but the Tumlinson group prevailed, nevertheless. The fight resulted in the death of all but one of the raiders, with none of the avenging party suffering injuries.

The Texas Rangers consider Tumlinson the first of their ranks to die in the line of duty on July 6, 1823. The Tumlinson sons now had a personal vendetta, which would play out in several different ways in the coming years.

Stephen Austin Returns

Austin's absence was a year-long, but he did, at last, return, with all the arrangements made for his colony's legal establishment. The fortunes of the settlers turned quickly around, for Austin was a man who believed in peaceful industry and the perseverance of hard work and encouraged the same in his colony by being highly selective of the people or families to whom he granted land. He would not, for example, grant land to anyone without a steady occupation or the income to get a good start. He had anyone of "bad character" escorted from the colonies, and those few paid for the privilege of this escort with their possessions.

Austin's methods showed his legal training and understanding; out of many empresarios, he was far and away from the most successful at relatively and legally distributing the land denoted to him by the Mexican government. It did take until 1824 for James Tumlinson, still head of his family, and John Jackson Tumlinson, Sr. 's widow, Elizabeth, to be granted their titles, but this was due to the delays caused by the confusion of the Mexican government and were beyond Austin's control. For his part, Austin was able to act as an effective go-between when his colonists, still "American" in their thinking (a trait which would never change), needed help in understanding how to deal with Mexican law and customs.

Those who can trace their ancestry to the Old 300 have good reason to be proud. The colonists' efforts were so successful that within a decade, they had created a thriving community amid a wilderness that had been avoided and unused by its stewards for the past several centuries. Under Austin's stewardship, profitable trade was established, attracting professionals and craft workers to Austin's settlement. Travel improved with the addition of roads, with ferries put in place to ease crossing the many rivers. Austin's colony was such a valuable addition to Texas that the Mexican government gave him the right to settle an additional nine hundred families over the next several years.

As the empresario, Austin was responsible for the protection of his colonists. He supported the hiring of rangers (and he was the first to use the job title in describing them) for the common defense of the families that had settled under his care. Austin paid the rangers not in cash but with land, of which he had plenty to give; he also commissioned the hiring of another ten men to join the ranks of the small group already formed.

Santa Anna

The governing power of Mexico was in for a hard run. Policy and power changed routinely, and sometimes violently, over the next decade. Search the history of the Mexican emperor and the presidents who followed, and one name will repeatedly appear as a critical influence, that of General Antonio López de Santa Anna. From the perspective of Texas, Santa Anna is infamous as the brutal aggressor in the Battle at the Alamo. Sam Houston and his army then defeated the General's forces at the Battle of San Jacinto, the deciding battle in the Texan Revolution.

However, those events were still years away. Santa Anna long had his hand in the story of Texas. His conveniently changing political position put him in place with power enough to start a war. While we focus on the Tumlinson family as they established their homesteads along the Colorado and Brazos Rivers, joining up with ranging companies to protect the colonists from Native attacks, it is essential to remember that the background of the swiftly tilting Mexican government was Santa Anna. He moved with purpose through one leader after another, one rebellion after another, with an uncanny knack for choosing the winning side of the fight, promoting his self-interests along the way.

The Mexican Empire

Santa Anna joined the Spanish military in 1810 when he was only 16 years old. During the Mexican Revolution, he fought on Spain's side against the Mexican rebellion and received quick promotions and commendations, making the rank of a first lieutenant by 1812. The Mexican Revolution simmered and sparked until in 1821, when Augustin de Iturbide, a royalist, switched sides and allied with the insurgents. Santa Anna switched sides, along with Iturbide, and now fought for Mexican independence. This is by no means the last time Santa Anna would "switch sides" in a fight.

Iturbide took control as Emperor of Mexico but had a short-lived reign. Santa Anna led a rebellion against Iturbide in 1822 when the emperor withdrew his promise of Santa Anna's "prize," the command of the Veracruz port. Santa Anna's rebellion was not successful, but it opened the door for further revolts, which eventually forced Iturbide off the throne. Iturbide surrendered in 1823 and left for Italy. Indeed, he would never have returned to Mexico had he realized that a firing squad awaited him. Federalists captured him trying to reenter the country at Soto la Marina the following summer and executed the former emperor.

The Death of Thomas Carney Tumlinson

Records aren't clear on the exact cause of death for John Jackson Tumlinson, Sr.'s oldest son, Thomas, indicating only that he died a "violent death." Family history, however, maintains that he died at the hands of Native aggressors. Even after so many Tumlinsons moved southward to Texas, Thomas remained in Arkansas. Presumably, he had a family there. At roughly the same time, his death occurred that his father died on the

Guadalupe River in Texas (summer of 1823). This tragedy certainly would have done nothing to improve the family's bitter feelings about Native tribes.

1824: The Republic of Mexico

Federalism versus Centralism

Amidst the conflict of these two opposing party viewpoints, Federalism and Centralism, Mexico became a republic in 1824. The difference between the groups is apparent in their names. The Centralists believed in a strong, central Mexican government with little power given to individual Mexican states, a united paid military force, and the ongoing rule of Mexican noble classes in practice, if not in theory – and more relevantly here, the Centralists disapproved of the massive influx of previously American citizens into their land. Of the two parties, the closer to Mexico's roots of imperialism and a far more comfortable fit for the upper classes.

The Federalists adopted a more "American" approach, welcoming immigrants, embracing the uneducated and poor of Mexico with equal rights (aiming to better their lives in the process), giving the majority of power to individual states, and functioning much as the United States did with a pretty similar constitution. This was, at least, their claim. However, the Federalists were not above ignoring the results of the legal election when the outcome did not suit them.

The fledgling Mexican government created its constitution, which enacted the empresario system, allowing each of the nineteen Mexican states to oversee its public lands by designating land managers, or "empresarios," with civil and military authority their regions. Stephen F. Austin received the empresario title for the property and the colonists covered under his land grant. Austin's colonists and most European/American immigrants, under Austin's jurisdiction or not, were firmly in favor of the Federalist viewpoint, as it so clearly suited their ambitions to populate and utilize the Texas wilderness.

Upon establishing the Republic of Mexico, Federalist Santa Anna made himself indispensable by offering his military force's services to protect critical Mexican states.

The State of Coahuila y Tejas

The Mexican Constitution of 1824 also joined the state of Texas with that of Coahuila, as neither area, in itself, possessed sufficient population for statehood. This joining formed the new state of Coahuila y Tejas, with its government seat in Saltillo. From that point until its separation many years later, this joining was a source of conflict. Coahuila, underpopulated as it might have been, still vastly outnumbered Texas in citizens and, therefore, consistently outvoted them on essential matters before congress, favoring the side of traditional Mexican nobility. The difference only reinforced the belief of the Texians that they were unheard of by the Mexican government.

The General Colonization Law

In 1824, the new Republic of Mexico also passed the General Colonization Law. This law permitted foreigners to obtain land titles and exempted them from taxes for ten years, provided their land was not less than 20 leagues from the border of another country or within ten leagues of the coast.

The passing of this law catalyzed a migration of American colonists to Coahuila y Tejas so massive that it naturally brought along a strong-minded version of "American Life," which would prove unwilling to bend its thinking its new country's ways. The philosophical difference would not remain one of thought alone and would, in a few years, have Mexico regretting its decision and backpedaling, trying desperately to shackle what was out of control. But by then, it was simply too late.

The First Mexican Election

Insurgent General Victoria, a Federalist, was the first president of the Republic of Mexico, elected in 1824 without trouble. Meanwhile, in Santa Anna's home state of Veracruz, Santa Anna was promoted to the position of lieutenant governor.

In 1827, the governor of Veracruz decided to side with rebels against the liberals in yet another rebellion attempt. This was the Montaño rebellion, which had a strange, masonic conflict in its making, its purpose of driving "secret societies" out of Mexico. Whatever the causes, Santa Anna was sympathetic to the rebellion, but he chose to fight for the liberals. When the rebels were defeated, this careful choice conveniently allowed him to step into the position as Veracruz's governor.

No More Easy Pickings

Meanwhile, in Texas y Coahuila, on the Brazos and Colorado Rivers, Stephen Austin's colony continued to flourish with little or no help from the Mexican government. Austin's steadfast leadership and the colonists' resolve were turning this former "wilderness" into a burgeoning economy and society surrounding the growing prosperous town of San Felipe de Austin.

The ranging companies led by Morrison and Kuykendall had significantly decreased raids. Whether the aggressors were Native tribes, criminal elements that had migrated south with the colonists, or others indigents of Mexico looking for easy pickings, the ferocity of the ranging companies strongly discouraged that behavior.

For some time in the early 1820s, one of the great dangers to colonists was the very last leg of travel to their new colony. Ships transported colonists from New Orleans to the port at the mouth of the Brazos. Ocean travel was generally preferable to the overland journey. Because Mexican law allowed no colonists to live within ten leagues of the coast, their destination of San Felipe de Austin still required an expedition north from the port to the colony. These wide-eyed colonists who carried all their worldly goods on hand made convenient targets. Tales were rampant of possessions and people completely disappearing in this "no man's land" between the sea and safety. One of the significant duties of the ranging companies was to discourage the idea that a virtual buffet of exhausted, overloaded travelers was available wandering north from the coast toward San Felipe.

With the Colonization Law in effect and the ranging companies on guard, the population continued growing.

Chapter Three:

Fears of Mexico

Visitors from Mexico City

After only three years of the Colonization Law in full effect in Texas, word reached Mexico City that their plan might be too successful. Texians were overtaking the economy and culture of their corner of this Mexican state, having brought powerful American ideology with them. In 1827, under the auspices of scientific research and verifying the Sabine and Red Rivers boundary, the Mexican government sent the Boundary Commission to Texas y Coahuila to assess the situation. Under wraps, the "situation" to consider was the actual number and the real motives of these colonials.

General Mier y Teran, mineralogist Rafael Chovell, cartographer Jos Maria Sanches y Tapia, and a Swiss botanist and zoologist named Jean Louis Berlandier comprised the Commission. They left Mexico City on November 1, 1827, and arrived in San Antonio de Bexar on March 1, 1828. Berlandier was overwhelmed with admiration for the botanical bounty of the area, particularly considering their arrival was technically at the tail end of the winter season, but his companions were not as enthusiastic. The living conditions of the population there dismayed them. They found Bexar's citizenry to be impoverished and uneducated farmers, constantly hassled by Natives.

The Commission then moved on to San Felipe de Austin by April 27, 1828, where they found a much different situation: a thriving colony improving the region's economic conditions. Worse, Tejanos had grown dependent on the Texians, not the other way around. Stephen Austin, himself, was polite to the Commission, though the relations between them were never overly friendly.

General Teran conceded that Austin's colony seemed to follow Mexican law as well as they could understand it. However, the Americanization of the area disturbed him. The Commission last visited Nacogdoches, where General Teran discovered the Tejanos living with many Americanized customs. When he saw his people emulating the colonists, he considered it a threat to his country's value system.

Tejanos, for their part, were mainly happy to be in the company of Texians for several reasons. First, Texas had always only served as a buffer between Mexico and the Comancheria to the west and the United States to the east. Tejanos felt their government owed them a debt of gratitude, in fact, but none was forthcoming. The literal distance and the sociological separation were too great. Thus detached from their government, Tejanos had fended for themselves and developed their own culture. American colonists had brought trade, safety, and previously unknown prosperity to the area.

Many months passed before General Teran, and his Commission returned to Mexico City with their report. Historically speaking, the Boundary Commission report provided some of the most valuable scientific information the government had ever acquired, but that was not the real purpose of the trip. General Teran returned with warnings that American values and customs were overrunning Texas, and by 1830, his recommendations to curb immigration would receive attention and action.

Napoleon of the West

In 1828, the Mexican presidential election was quite tense. Santa Anna supported the insurgency hero Vincente Guerrero in Guerrero's bid for president. The election results, unfortunately, gave the victory to Centralist Manuel Pedraza. Though he had fought for the Mexican republic with "free elections" as part of the deal, Santa Anna issued a plan that called for the nullification of the election. His efforts gained support until President-Elect Pedraza fled the country. Guerrero took office, and Santa Anna gained national fame as a defender for Federalism.

In 1829, Spain invaded. In a final attempt to retake Mexico, forces entered the country through the port at Tampico. President Guerrero sent Santa Anna to turn back this Spanish invasion. Santa Anna defeated the Spaniards, even with a much smaller force (luckily for him, many of the Spanish soldiers were ill with yellow fever at the time). Santa Anna's victory at Tampico made him a national hero. He called himself "The Napoleon of the West."

President Guerrero did not fare so well. When Spain invaded, he enacted emergency executive powers. Although Santa Anna defeated the invading force, Guerrero refused to rescind these emergency executive powers, and it was not long before his gambit caused the authorities to turn against him.

In December 1829, Mexico's Vice-President, Anastasio Bustamante (a Centralist), rebelled against President Guerrero. President Guerrero left the capitol, rushing south, and Bustamante took over the presidency in January of 1830. As it was a primary goal of Centralism, Bustamante wanted to enhance and enlarge the Mexican army and to do so. He needed a great deal of money.

Much of Bustamante's monies came from significantly increased taxes and additional sums his government borrowed from moneylenders. Funds went toward building up the military through new equipment and recruitment. The Mexican Army flourished, ready to take on the forces of Spain, should they return, and take action against the nebulous threat forming in Texas. In this once worthless corner, neglect from the Mexican government and the influx of American colonists had led to a problematic situation: success and power outside of Mexico's control.

On the Brazos and Colorado Rivers

The Death of Robert Kuykendall

In late 1830, ranger squad captain Robert Kuykendall was severely injured in a fight against Karankawa natives. A severe blow to the head left him blind and paralyzed. He technically survived the attack but did not survive subsequent trepanning as doctors attempted to reduce the swelling in his brain. He died at the age of 40.

By 1831, sons of John Jackson Tumlinson, Sr. (Andrew, John Jackson Jr., and Joseph) and James Tumlinson, Jr. (David, James III, and Littleton) acquired land in Green DeWitt's county. DeWitt was another successful empresario and friends with Stephen Austin. Together, DeWitt and Austin actively attempted to convince Mexican President Bustamante, through firm but polite correspondence, that their colonists acted in good faith toward the Mexican government.

Bustamante, nudged by the fears of Boundary Commission leader General Teran, busily enacted decrees to stop and disempower the American colonists. He issued the Law of April 6, 1830, which forbids any further immigration into Texas and canceled unfinished empresario contracts. American colonists could continue to settle anywhere else in Mexico – just not in Texas.

Tejanos were as displeased with the law as Texians and Americans. They wanted no interference that would drive Americans away. Though Texian and Tejano, culture did not live together, as Tejanos grouped mainly around San Antonio de Bexar, Nacogdoches, and Victoria-Goliad. In contrast, Texians lived around San Felipe de Austin and the Brazos River's fertile land, the Tejanos, nevertheless, relied heavily on the prosperity of their Texian neighbors. Whatever prejudices existed between the two peoples, money and safety trumped their differences.

Bustamante pushed trade between Texas and other Mexican states in hopes of diminishing the United States' commercial influence. He tried (without much success) to get Europeans and especially other Mexicans to settle in Texas to counterbalance the exploding American-based population. Finally, Bustamante began transferring Mexican troops to Texas to support his measures.

The Tumlinson Cannon

The capital of Green DeWitt's colony was Gonzales (named respectfully after the acting governor of Coahuila y Tejas). The capitol, established in 1825, suffered two devastating Native attacks before DeWitt moved what remained of the place to a safer location.

In 1831, DeWitt sent a letter to the Political Chief Músquiz in San Antonio de Bexar. In this message, he requested to "borrow" a cannon for the town's defense. Natives feared cannons, and the possession of one was a powerful deterrent. Músquiz granted the request, providing a small Spanish bronze six-pounder (i.e., it would fire six-pound cannonballs) for DeWitt's use.

James Tumlinson, Jr., of the Old 300, owned sizable property and a freighting business in Gonzales and had three sons with land grants in DeWitt's County. He originally lived in the Columbus colony with his family but relocated to DeWitt's colony after his first wife's death. James Tumlinson, Jr., took possession of the cannon in San Antonio de Bexar and returned safely with it to Gonzales.

Please do not be mistaken because it was no coincidence that the bronze cannon was signed for and retrieved by James Tumlinson, Jr., and later possibly hidden and buried by the Tumlinson family. Years before, John Jackson Tumlinson, Sr., the first alcalde of the Columbus colony and co-founder of the Texas Rangers, died at the hands of Native Americans. The Tumlinson's are believable to have considered the cannon's presentation to their colony a gesture in recognition of John Jackson Tumlinson, Sr. 's ultimate sacrifice to his country. You can imagine what an insult it was to them in later years when the Mexican government wanted it back.

DeWitt and Músquiz agreed that DeWitt's colony would return the cannon if ever requested by the Mexican government. However, by the time Mexico did request the return of this little cannon, Green DeWitt was dead, and whether his colonists were aware of his promise, no one ever knew.

For the time being, the cannon would sit as the deterrent it was meant to be, unfired—and possibly even not fully assembled—until the request for its return provided the spark for the first conflict in the Texas Revolution.

The Death of Andrew Tumlinson

In the years following John Jackson Tumlinson, Sr. 's murder on the Guadalupe, his son, Andrew, took every possible opportunity to lead expeditions to track down and kill Natives. Often, he left his wife and their child in the care of her brother while he went absent for long stretches to pursue revenge. His hatred for the tribes of Texas was well-known. His date of death is not – records aren't specific but narrow its occurrence to either 1830 or early 1831.

The story of his demise is a grim one. A native man discovered trespassing on a settler's property refused to explain his reasons for being there. Andrew's expedition took the man into custody to return with him to the settlement and conduct further investigation. Andrew, however, was not willing to wait. The Native was huddled beneath a blanket and had surrendered his rifle – yet still refused to uncover himself or stand. Against the recommendations of his comrades, Andrew approached the Native, intent on questioning the man himself. When Andrew was close enough, the Native drew a blade and attacked. Andrew had enough time to shoot the Native, but his falling opponent stabbed him several times before both men lay dead on the ground, two more lives claimed in the quest for vengeance.

Had Andrew survived, he almost certainly would have joined his younger brothers, John Jackson Jr., Joseph, and Peter, as they participated in the Texas Revolution, for outright rebellion was on the horizon. As with all the events leading up to the Texas Revolution and the fight itself, the Tumlinsons were always close at hand.

Peter Tumlinson Returns to Texas

Peter, another son of John Jackson, Sr. and Elizabeth Tumlinson, had come to Texas with his family in 1821. He returned to Tumlinson Township in Arkansas in 1823, though it is uncertain whether he went before or after the murder of his father. In Arkansas, Peter married Tennie Tidwell, and they had three sons before Tennie's death.

Records are sketchy about the fate of Peter and Tennie's first son. Still, their second and third sons, Absolom and William, would later distinguish themselves in the service of the Texas Rangers, notably under their father's command (along with a third son, Joseph, born from Peter's second marriage), defending the Rio Grande frontier during the Cortina "disturbances" in 1859.

Though the precise date of his return is unknown (records place his arrival anywhere from 1830 to 1835), Peter rejoined his family in Texas just in time for the oncoming revolution. He volunteered to serve in the Texas Army's cavalry division under Captain Hooper's San Augustine Company.

Peter Tumlinson's return to Texas may be a matter of some mystery, but that same quality suits the times well. From 1830 to 1835, conditions between Texian immigrants and the Mexican Government were unstable, wavering back and forth from violence to concession and back again. Stephen Austin did his best to maintain control over the population, but American sentiment quickly rebelled against any overassertive authority. The Mexican Government did little to help the situation with its ever-changing politics and military intimidation.

Santa Anna's Next Move

In Mexico City, President Bustamante pleased most of the legislature (i.e., the powerful nobility) by imposing Centralist values on the Republic of Mexico. His actions included more than just bolstering troops to deal with the troublesome American population in Tejas y Coahuila. Bustamante's government performed numerous political arrests, and he even developed a secret police force to root out dissent. However, in 1831, Bustamante took matters too far.

Centralist forces captured (or some might say, "kidnapped") former President Guerrero, who was still in exile from the capitol. They executed Guerrero before a firing squad, an event that horrified Mexican citizens. Despite everything, Guerrero was a hero of the Mexican Revolution. Public opinion of Bustamante lowered to the point that Santa Anna's subsequent actions met with little opposition.

Thus, that same year, Santa Anna declared himself to be in open rebellion against Bustamante. He seized control of the tax revenues from Veracruz and went to Mexico City, where he led a violent coup against Bustamante's government. However, it took him the better part of a year to accomplish his ultimate goal.

War Dogs

While Santa Anna moved through his own machinations in Mexico City, a fiery brand of Texians made their own plans. With no particular inception, a rabble-rousing crowd of discontent colonists came together beginning roughly in 1827. They did not call themselves "War Dogs" or "The War Party", but their opponents, including Stephen Austin, certainly did. This small group of men, whose numbers were at most around two dozen associates, worked covertly to advance their own agenda. They disagreed with Stephen Austin's peaceful accommodation of the Mexican government. They desired affiliation with Mexico, but not with Mexican laws or taxes – though this begs the question of exactly what they expected from such a bargain.

Several famous names filled the ranks of the War Dogs. While the ringleaders of the group were brothers John and William Wharton, they drew to their ranks Robert "Three-Legged Willie" Williamson (who would become a famous Texas Ranger, serving as their first Major), James Bowie, and Sam Houston. In fact, the Whartons invited Sam Houston to Texas in 1832. Thanks to a rowdy reputation and an affinity for drinking, Houston had burned a few bridges in the United States. Texas was an excellent place to start anew, which is exactly what the Whartons invited Sam Houston to do.

Over the years, the War Dogs organized various small militia groups, published editorials berating the Mexican government, and represented a discontent faction of the population at the conventions of 1832 and 1833. They were the most outspoken and active of the colonists, the face of a stream of dissatisfaction with the impositions of their government. This much is clear: they felt Mexico had no right to rule them.

Presidios in Texas

As the leader of the Boundary Commission, General Teran was Bustamante's best source of information on the alarming prosperity – and numbers – of the Texian colonists. The General, therefore, returned to Texas under Bustamante's orders, this time with military backing, instead of a mere research team. There, he built up the forces of the Mexican Army to impede immigration. General Teran ordered that several presidios (basically, forts) be erected to keep a close watch on the happenings in Texas and keep the colonists under control. This measure led to a series of rebellions known as the Anahuac Disturbances. However, the fights took place not only in Anahuac but in Velasco and Nacogdoches, the latter two uprisings inspired by the first one.

The presidio at Anahuac, a port town near Galveston Bay, served to watch trade and prevent smuggling from

Louisiana to Texas. General Teran put Juan Bradburn in charge. Though Bradburn was initially from America, he showed no patience nor sympathy toward immigrants and was highly paranoid (perhaps justifiably) of immigrant conspiracy. His control over the presidio, and therefore, the town, was unexpectedly rigid. Many of his soldiers were Mexican prisoners who chose military service instead of prison time, so violence was more often their answer to the trouble.

American immigrants were a proud bunch, unwilling to suffocate under what they considered an authoritarian rule. They rose in several acts of civil disobedience, including vandalism and confrontations with Bradburn's mercenary soldiers. Anglo citizens drafted up the "Turtle Bayou Resolutions," in which they claimed to support Santa Anna and the 1824 Constitution, a direct slap in the face of the Centralist regime.

In June of 1832, Bradburn arrested two Anglo attorneys who were busily trying to incite rebellion to keep control. Local insurgents "rescued" the attorneys in a scuffle that resulted in the deaths of five Centralist soldiers and one Anglo colonist. Bradburn feared that he was losing his presidio and sent to Nacogdoches for help.

Colonel Piedras of the Nacogdoches garrison responded. He came to Anahuac with 100 troops to negotiate with the Anglo population. He offered concessions – namely the resignation of Juan Bradburn. The Anglo population accepted. Piedras restored order in Anahuac by early July 1832.

Anahuac was not the only presidio attacked. Residents of Brazoria, with a schooner and one cannon, seized another of General Teran's presidios, Fort Velasco. That "disturbance" was surprisingly bloody, resulting in several deaths. Mexican troops unequipped to deal with raiders surrendered and abandoned the garrison.

All seemed to be well as Colonel Piedras made the return trip to Nacogdoches; unfortunately, word of the colonist uprising reached Nacogdoches before he did. With the inspiration of Anahuac and Velasco, the Anglos of Nacogdoches marched on the Centralist's garrison, and a bloody fight broke out in the streets of the town and went on for days. Piedras and his garrison finally retreated toward San Antonio de Bexar on August 2. On the way there, they were intercepted by the so-called National Militia, led by James Bowie and James Bullock (one gets a sense of the War Dogs at work here). Bowie and Bullock forced Piedras to surrender.

With civil disobedience moving from the printed word to bloody street fighting, Centralist forces moved out of Eastern Texas. Cooler heads prevailed, however. Stephen Austin, still the most respected man in the Anglo colonies scorned insurgent behavior. He believed that peaceful resolution to the dispute was always the preferred method and that a solution to this discord would be found across a negotiation table.

Two Conventions

The Convention of 1832

Negotiations began – or were somewhat clumsily attempted – starting in 1832 as Texians held two conventions in San Felipe de Austin, one in August of 1832 (presided over by a doubtful Stephen Austin, who felt that the convention was happening too soon for it to do any real good), and another a few months later, in April of 1833. Texian representatives from the ayuntamientos (town councils) of Anglo-colonized Texas attended both conventions. Fifty-eight representatives participated at the first convention, and fifty-six participated at the second. Though invited to attend, Tejano ayuntamientos largely refused to take part.

Texians wanted the following:
1. The separation of Texas from Coahuila
2. An end to the immigration ban
3. Exemptions from customs duty until 1835; and
4. The ability to remove "corrupt" customs officials.

Both conventions saw documents drafted to this effect. Why, then, were there two conventions for the same purpose? The problem with the first convention was twofold. First, while friendly to the colonists' cause, political chief Ramon Musquiz of Bexar informed them that the "convention" was not an acceptable method of hammering out their irritations with the government; this presumptiveness would only anger the Mexican legislature. He vetoed their drafted petition before it ever left Texas. Secondly, Mexico's government underwent yet another abrupt change, forcing Bustamante out of office. These combined reasons rendered the first convention irrelevant, much as Stephen Austin had predicted.

President Santa Anna
After months of conflict, far south in Mexico City, Bustamante finally resigned from the office of Mexican

President in December of 1832. Santa Anna, who still claimed to be a Federalist, cleverly restored Centralist Gomez Pedraza to President's office. This made Santa Anna look magnanimous, somehow, even though although Pedraza had legally won the election in 1828, Santa Anna had been vital in denying Pedraza the presidency. Political memories seemed to have a short life in Mexico City.

But Santa Anna could afford to let Pedraza take office now because part of Bustamante's surrender agreement was that a new presidential election would be held in 1833. Santa Anna ran as a Federalist and easily won.

Santa Anna was fond of titles and was more than happy to accept that of President. He did not, however, wish to involve himself in governing. Instead of returning to his home in Veracruz, he spent little time in Mexico City to leave the running of the government to his Vice President Valentín Gómez Farías.

The Second Convention

Santa Anna's election was good news to the Texians. They hurriedly put together the plans for their *second* convention. Was luck on their side this time? They believed that Federalist President Santa Anna would be sympathetic to their cause. Because the War Dogs were heading the convention this time, with William Wharton leading, instead of the far more levelheaded Austin, the tone was much changed. This time, they would not permit Mexican bureaucracy to stop them from presenting their case before Mexico City. If Mexico City did not hear them, they would take action on their own.

Sam Houston led the committee that drafted a constitution much like that of the United States. Stephen Austin agreed to take it to Mexico City. Plans fell through for those who were to accompany him, so Austin had to make the journey alone. He dreaded the trip, though he could not have known the trouble that awaited him. He would not return to Texas for two-and-a-half years.

The Trials of Stephen Austin

Cholera and Seasickness

Austin contracted cholera soon after he left for Mexico City. He managed to recover but was in such a weakened state that he could not travel overland. Though Austin despised sea travel, he had no choice except to book passage on a boat to Veracruz. Rough weather beset his entire voyage. What should have taken a week took a month. Austin was seasick the whole time.

When, at last, he arrived in the capitol in July of 1833, Santa Anna was not there. Austin met with Vice President Farías, whose liberal leanings gave Austin hope that the Texians would be heard, though Mexican congress was still unwilling to open negotiations with the Texians. Then, while Austin was in Mexico City, the rampant cholera epidemic struck and brought all business to a stop. Once more, Austin became ill. This time, he almost died.

By October 1833, a depressed and sickened Austin wrote to Bexar, stating that the ongoing civil war being Federalism and Centralism made business dealings impossible, and nothing more could be accomplished. He said that he believed Texas should unite as a government independent of Coahuila.

However, Santa Anna's return to the city resulted in what Austin perceived as a much-improved situation. He and Santa Anna got along well in the two meetings they shared, and Austin was able to get Santa Anna's cooperation. Santa Anna promised to revoke the immigration law and reinstate the empresario system (this would occur the following year, resulting in a new influx of settlers from the United States). As for the Texians' other demands, these went unmet. Still, in December of 1833, Austin left the city with lightened spirits, feeling he had done all he could.

Arrested

On January 2, 1834, Stephen Austin arrived in Saltillo on his journey home, arrested for treason. Whatever his intentions were, the contents of the letter he wrote in October seemed so radical that his associates in Bexar had turned the correspondence over to the government so they would not be seen as complicit. With a military escort, Austin returned to Mexico City. There, an inquisition prison held him for three months.

In the months that followed, Austin would be transferred to better accommodations and even finally released on bail. Still, he was not permitted to leave Mexico City as the Mexican courts bandied his case back and forth, attempting to determine precisely what law he had broken and under whose jurisdiction the matter came.

Farías at the Helm

Mexican Vice President Farías, left in charge as President Santa Anna enjoyed a leisurely presidency in Veracruz (temporarily at least), had to contend with the serious issue of an empty treasury. President Bustamante had left the nation with an 11 million peso debt. Without another possible source of income, Farías seized the non-essential property and possessions of the Roman Catholic Church, cutting their power over education and tithing. Of course, this enraged the church and angered Mexican conservatives. At Santa Anna's suggestion, Farías also initiated cuts in military spending, reducing battalions and officers.

Santa Anna's plans are unclear at this point, but it is plausible that he allowed, and even encouraged, Farías to run a "test" of how well a liberal Mexican government would be received. Leaving Farías at the head of liberal reform gave Santa Anna a measure of plausible deniability if things went severely but allowed Santa Anna to take credit under his presidency if things went well. Things did not go well. Centralist rebellions rose against the liberal reform, even in Santa Anna's home province of Veracruz.

* * *

Santa Anna Switches Sides

Resistance from the great powers of the Church and the army was too much for the liberal government. They saw Farías's reforms as radical. Farías had been set up to take a fall. In 1834, Santa Anna (until quite recently a liberal Federalist) returned to office, declaring that the government was hereafter Centralist, conservative, and Catholic. He repudiated his support of the 1824 Constitution. He repealed all liberal reforms that Farías had issued and driven the poor vice president into exile.

The Catholic Church paid for the right to have its powers returned – which, in effect, solved Mexico's money problem. Santa Anna filled congress with clergy and military representatives. Santa Anna replaced the Republic of Mexico's 1824 constitution with the Seven Laws constitutional document, a series of laws that promoted all the Centralist ideals: a powerful central government, a robust central military, with little power afforded to the Mexican states. He formed a standing national army, meaning that soldiers were now loyal to Mexico City (and thus, to Santa Anna), and he drastically reduced state militias. By January of 1835, the Mexican congress met with a Centralist majority. Mexico lauded Santa Anna once more for being a national savior, this time for upholding traditional and religious values.

When Federalist states rebelled against these changes, Santa Anna's reprisals were brutal. The most infamous example of his revenge was the Sack of Zacatecas. After quelling that state's rebellion, Santa Anna allowed his soldiers to pillage the capital city, also called Zacatecas, for two days. One can only imagine the results. Fear spread throughout the country, eliminating further attempts at resistance. Then, the Centralist government turned its eyes back to collecting taxes from the rapidly expanding population of Texas.

Chapter Four:

Come and Take It

1835

For over a decade, growing tensions between Texians and Mexico City politics resulted in skirmishes, negotiations, broken promises, and broken laws. Finally, in 1835, events aligned that set Texians on an unstoppable course.

- Santa Anna's Centralist government was in control and ready to tax the burgeoning Texian population.
- Texians already had a standing grudge against the Centralist military (i.e., the Anahuac Disturbances).
- Their hero, Stephen Austin, was being held as a prisoner in Mexico City.
- Austin's faith in the Mexican government wavered severely as a result of his treatment.

Things were about to get noisy in Texas. Before we move on to the noise, however, we must take note of an essential event in the history of Texas law enforcement.

Formal Inception

In 1835, what had previously been a militia of ranging volunteers became an officially constituted law enforcement company. Members earned $1.25 a day, the same pay as an army sergeant. Their first major was Robert "Three-Legged Willie" Williamson. Williamson's oddball nickname came from wearing a prosthetic device to support his malformed, though not missing, right leg – permanently bent at the knee because of a childhood illness.

Captain Tumlinson – The First Ranger Captain

Williamson organized three authorized Ranger companies, making John Jackson Tumlinson, Jr. the captain of one, its duty to protect and patrol the Anglo-American settlements in Williamson County. Because his ranging company saw active service before the other two, John Jackson, Jr. is considered the "first" captain of an official Texas Ranger company. His company's adventures put them directly in the middle of the first steps of revolution.

More Trouble in Anahuac

Once more, the port town of Anahuac became the center of the dispute, as a radical group calling themselves the Citizens of Texas accused corrupt officials of taking money off the top of collected customs. Civil disobedience drama played out almost exactly as before: two outspoken rebels, both local businessmen, were taken into custody after they "pranked" port commander Antonio Tonorio by filling his ship with nothing but ballast. Soon after the men were taken into Centralist custody, a local Texian militia group, consisting of 25 men and a cannon, arrived to demand their release. Not coincidentally, because he had a symbolic ax to grind, William Barret Travis led this militia. Travis was one of the two men who had been imprisoned during Anahuac's earlier disturbance of 1832.

A Changed Man

Texians were out of patience with the impermanence and disregard of the Mexican Government. Santa Anna's violent retributions toward those who dared oppose him concerned Texians seriously. They feared being his next target.

The majority of Texians would probably have continued under Stephen Austin's policy of adjusting peacefully to the new country, except that Stephen Austin had been taken from them. What's more, during the long months he was forbidden to leave Mexico City, Austin's view of the Mexican Government soured. He saw what Santa Anna was doing to the country. The immigration ban had been lifted, that much was true, and Austin had hoped that the massive immigration of Anglos would sufficiently Americanize Texas so that the Mexican Government would have no choice but to cooperate with and respect them. Yet, his correspondence to San Felipe de Austin (fortunately not intercepted this time) began to sound more like the writings of the War Dogs than those of his previous, patient self.

By July of 1835, Mexican courts finally closed the perplexing case against Austin using a loophole. They ruled that he had the amnesty of a political prisoner and released him. He left for home on July 11. The return trip took Austin two long voyages – first to New Orleans and then to Brazoria – and one sea battle, when his ship, the *San Felipe*, engaged and captured Mexican revenue cutter *Correa de Mexico*. At last, he returned to the town that bore his name. During that first week of September 1835, the Texians joyfully celebrated their homecoming of their respected leader.

But during the months Austin endeavored to return, Texas rumbled with sounds of defiance. The Commandant General of the Eastern Interior Provinces, General Martin Perfecto de Cos, issued warrants for the arrest of William Barret Travis (who had led the latest rebellion in Anahuac), Three-Legged William Williamson (Major of the Texas Rangers), and several other popular Texians.

The Texians informed General Cos that they would release none of their citizens to him, nor to anyone else in the Mexican Government, and not to put too fine a point on their view, called him a Centralist toady. Soon, dispatches arrived with terrible news: General Cos was bringing a Centralist army to Texas. In response, Texians throughout the region organized safety committees. A hasty plan came together for a General Consultation in the town of Washington on the Brazos in October.

On September 20, General Cos and 500 Centralist soldiers landed in Copano to quell the rebellion. Instead, they incited it. Stephen Austin, the last significant holdout for the hope of peaceful coexistence, proclaimed that attempts to conciliation were now pointless. War was the only answer.

Come and Take It

Since 1831, the bronze cannon had done its simple job, acting as a deterrent against any who might consider raiding Gonzales. It had never been fired; it had not even been completely assembled.

The town of Gonzales was not interested in the brewing rebellion. In July of 1835, they sent correspondence to Colonel Domingo de Ugartechea, commander of the Presidio San Antonio de Bexar. In their message, the citizens of Gonzales pledged continued loyalty to the Mexican government, a desire for peace, but a "suggestion" that Mexico City should not dispatch Centralist soldiers to Texas. Colonel Ugartechea, for his part, had enjoyed an excellent working arrangement with Green DeWitt and so maintained a reasonably good relationship with the people of Gonzales. Quite recently, the town's citizens had assisted his soldiers in pursuing Native raiders in the region.

Misunderstanding broke this tentative peace. On September 9, mere days following the return of Stephen Austin to Texas, a company of Centralist soldiers entered Gonzales and "occupied" the general store. A local man tried to enter the premises, failing to understand it was under temporary military command. The Centralists struck him over the head and threw him right back out again.

Andrew Ponton, the alcalde of Gonzales, wrote a polite but unhappy letter to Ugartechea, protesting the assault on a Gonzales citizen. In response, or rather more in lack of response, Ugartechea dispatched soldiers to Gonzales to get his little six-pounder cannon back.

Green DeWitt died the previous May, and along with him, any knowledge of the agreement he had made with Ugartechea (precisely, that the cannon was only being "borrowed" from Mexico). The citizens of Gonzales were not pleased to hear that Mexico planned to take away the cannon, their town's best means of protection. Rather than willingly hand it over, they buried the cannon in an orchard. When the unsuspecting Corporal De Leon and his soldiers of the Second Flying Company of San Carlos entered Gonzales to retrieve Mexico's property, they found themselves arrested and imprisoned.

Ugartechea then sent 100 troops under Captain Castaneda to retrieve both the cannon and the prisoners. Indeed that number of soldiers would prove the seriousness of his demands. When the Mexican soldiers arrived at the Guadalupe River, they found all the ferries that might transport them across to Gonzales had been removed. Eighteen armed Gonzales men on the opposite river bank informed the Mexicans, none too politely, that they could wait there – no more Centralist soldiers would be entering their town.

The call to action spread quickly through nearby Texian settlements: the Centralists had come to rob Gonzales of the cannon. Soon, about 140 men from surrounding territories joined the Gonzales militia beside the Guadalupe, allegedly 300 more on the way from further out. One such group of 30 men was the Bastrop Company, led by Lieutenant John Jackson Tumlinson, Jr., who had taken over command when their captain, Robert Coleman, became ill. Several other famous names joined the group, including War Dog John Wharton, James Bowie, and Captain James Walker Fannin.

Mexican commander Castaneda heard of the enormous Texian response to the Centralist presence and ordered that his troops retreat. He had come to collect a cannon and some men, not to fight a battle.

In Gonzales, the proud and quite riled-up Texians held a council of war. If the Centralists retreated, the Texians would chase them down. They dug up the cannon and, with the help of volunteer gunsmith – and someday, Texas historian – Noah Smithwick, assembled it into working order on a makeshift wagon to be pulled by oxen. Without accurate ammunition available for the cannon, they used iron slugs hammered into balls.

Two women from Gonzales fashioned an unforgettable but straightforward six-foot flag to fly: the image of the cannon and a lone star on a field of white, with the daring words "COME AND TAKE IT" sewn below. The flag flew above the cannon during the battle. The fact that the English sentence likely meant nothing to Mexican soldiers was hardly an issue; the sentiment exploded a fighting spirit in the Texian troops.

In the early morning hours of October 2, the Texians crossed the Guadalupe and made their way into

Castaneda's camp. With them, they brought two cannons – the quickly assembled cannon and a smaller one. They had precisely two more cannons than did the Centralists, who were not ready to engage these mad-eyed colonials who had more firepower. When the Texians fired upon the Centralists, they killed two Centralist soldiers and several horses.

The Centralist troops did as Castaneda had planned: they retreated rapidly to San Antonio de Bexar. And, also as designed, the Texians flocking to Gonzales followed. The Mexican Army in San Antonio vastly outnumbered them, and countless Natives waited nearby, looking for any opportunity to swoop in to reclaim their hunting grounds. The Texians did not care. They would march from Gonzales to San Antonio, picking up more and more volunteers. They had no uniforms and few horses; only flintlock rifles and Bowie knives armed them. The cannon led the way as a symbol of their defiance, with its "Come and take it!" flag flying.

Provisional Government

Simultaneously with the march to San Antonio, Texian representatives scrambled to reach San Felipe to form a provisional government. The pressing business was to beckon volunteers to a Texian army and somehow to supply that army. In discussing this, however, the delegates realized that there was no agreed reason why they were fighting the Mexicans.

Were they immediately declaring independence from Mexico? No, the assembly was not ready to alienate the Tejanos. Were they coming out to oppose Santa Anna and the Centralists? No, this idea, too, was down-voted. Finally, the assembly agreed that Texas was a Federalist Mexican state fighting to restore Mexico's 1824 Constitution. It was Santa Anna's despotism that had driven them to violence. They drafted the document "The Declaration of the People of Texas" to state their purpose.

The assembly elected Henry Smith as governor, James Robinson as lieutenant governor, and Sam Houston as major general of the Texas army. Soon, the problems of these appointments became apparent, as the rules and powers of these offices were poorly defined. When the time came to make decisions, no one indeed had the authority to do so. What's more, Sam Houston was the Major General of nothing at all – for Texas had no army to speak of, except the one marching on San Antonio de Bexar, and this rowdy crowd had already chosen another to lead them.

Volunteer Army of the People of Texas

Texian volunteers gathered by the hundreds, each group showing up with its captain or commander. Squabbling over command ensued until the arrival of Stephen Austin, who was nominated to be commander in chief. Austin, still immensely weakened from his illnesses, extended imprisonment, and recent travels did not want the position. Nevertheless, they unanimously elected him. It seemed he was the only one who could rally the soldiers together.

The Volunteer Army of the People of Texas set out from Gonzales on its march to San Antonio de Bexar on October 12. John Jackson Tumlinson, Jr. served as an advance scout. On October 16, John Jackson's squad captured a Mexican soldier who gave them valuable information about San Antonio's situation and forces.

General Cos had arrived in San Antonio with 400 men. About 800 reinforcements had come from Coahuila. With well over a thousand soldiers, Cos fortified the town for a defensive stand.

Though the Texians wanted to seize Bexar before more Centralist reinforcements could come, tearing a path through the settlements along the way, Stephen Austin could see that a frontal assault on Bexar was impossible. They had low numbers and no accurate artillery to speak of, save for the rallying sight of the little cannon and its lumpy lead cannonballs. With approach impossible, Austin decided to lay siege on the town, cutting off all its supplies until he forced the desperate Centralists to surrender. The siege lasted until December 5.

Skirmishes Outside San Antonio

While the siege went on, Stephen Austin sent James Bowie and Captain James Fannin to scout a better camp location, one from which the Texians could deflect Mexican troops or supply trains arriving to reinforce Bexar. Bowie and Fannin took ninety men (including John Jackson, Jr.) and traveled up the San Antonio River. After getting the lay of the land, they decided to set up a base in Mission Concepción. Though the location was a good one, their position was dangerous until the rest of the Volunteer Army could join them there.

General Cos's scouts discovered them. The general sent out Colonel Ugartechea and almost 300 Centralist soldiers to annihilate Bowie and Fannin's small reconnaissance group. Bowie had wisely placed sentries in positions to see any oncoming threats, and the river formed a natural barrier, which added to their safety. John Jackson, Jr. and the other Texians were able to pick off the Centralists as they approached. Within half an hour, the Centralist forces withdrew, and Austin arrived with the remainder of the Volunteer Army. The long odds of this victory caused a surge in Texian morale.

Less intense encounter, James Bowie, John Jackson, Jr., and their scouting companies encountered a mule supply train heading into Bexar. They attacked the supply train but found that it was only bringing in the grass for the starving animals inside the besieged town. This disruption was after that known as the "Grass Fight."

Austin's Last Try

The siege dragged on for weeks. Stephen Austin did not have the physical stamina to withstand the stress; meanwhile, the bored troops took to drinking. They drank so much that Austin begged San Felipe to stop sending alcohol with the army supplies. Then, as is often the case with crowded camps, illness began to spread through the men.

Politicians in San Felipe decided it might be better to relieve Austin of this position before killing him. He was appointed as an agent to the United States. Austin was only too happy to take the opportunity, but he did not wish to leave a job unfinished in his usual, meticulous fashion. On November 21, he ordered an assault on San Antonio.

Most of the Volunteer Army of the People of Texas refused. A flabbergasted Austin demanded to know if the siege should even continue. The troops decided that the blockade could go on under a new commander. The volunteers elected Edward Burleson, and Stephen Austin went gratefully back to San Felipe.

Edward Burleson also tried to order an assault on Bexar, and once more, the volunteers refused. The entire venture might have ended right there, with the army heading off to winter in Goliad, and who knows what repercussions for the State of Texas, had not Ben Milam spoken up.

Following Old Ben Milam

Benjamin Milam was an empresario whose adventures in Texas had been as uncertain and dangerous as many others. He, too, had sought to negotiate with the government, had been imprisoned, and had even escaped. During his escape, he met up with the Volunteer Army en route to San Antonio de Bexar and joined them.

On December 4, he saw the Volunteer Army readying to drift away from its cause to his dismay. He shouted down the complacent troops, shaming them into attacking San Antonio. He cried out to them, "Who will go with old Ben Milam into San Antonio?" Three hundred of the five hundred remaining troops agreed to attack San Antonio with him.

On December 5, Milam divided his force into two groups and snuck into the town, establishing a foothold. Then, relentlessly, the Volunteer Army took San Antonio house by house, street by street. It took five long and bloody days. "Old Ben Milam" did not survive the battle. A shot through the head killed him. His death drove his troops into a fervor of impassioned fighting.

General Cos finally surrendered and took his soldiers south of the Rio Grande. The victory left San Antonio de Bexar and all of Texas under Texian control. The triumphant Texians thought the war won and over.

Tumlinsons in the Siege of Bexar

During the Siege of Bexar, John Jackson, Jr. continued to act as an advanced scout. Thus, he and his squad were participants in the fight at the Mission Concepción and the Grass Fight, but they did not fight for the town's five-day battle. As the struggle inside San Antonio began, John Jackson, Jr.'s squad went out of the city to intercept Mexican reinforcements.

James Tumlinson's sons, George, James, Jr., and Littleton, all "followed old Ben Milam" into San Antonio. James, Jr., and Littleton were members of the Brazos Guards, who fought in both the Grass Fight and Mission Concepción. On the second day of the battle in San Antonio, their division seized and held a house on the advancing line of action, for that was the way they took the city: one house at a time.

The Fate of the Cannon

The proud "Come and take it!" flag was lost to history, but it and the bronze cannon were not forgotten by those roused to the cause. The cannon's ultimate fate is a matter of some debate, thanks to conflicting information from the records of the time and subsequent renditions of the march from Gonzales to Bexar.

Historian Dr. Patrick Wagner theorizes that the little cannon's impromptu repair and transport were insufficient to survive the march from Gonzales to San Antonio de Bexar. The Cannon was abandoned on the west side of Sandies Creek. It was even given a burial, perhaps out of a sense of respect, leaving its flag (after that lost) as a marker nearby. Over a century later, in 1936, a flood uncovered the cannon, and a local rescue worker found and transported the cannon to the Gonzales post office, where it remained for over three decades. It was only after the construction of a new post office, a lucky trade, and Dr. Wagner's spying on the cannon at the National Rifle Association display in San Antonio in 1979 that the history of the little cannon was investigated. Using x-ray technology and comparing the results against the records of Noah Smithwick and others, Dr. Wagner determined that this was the long-missing cannon. It is now displayed in the Gonzales Memorial Museum. This is the most widely accepted resolution.

Dr. Wagner's theory was roundly dismissed by Texas historian Thomas Ricks Lindley, who cites multiple sources that undermine the idea that the cannon was ever abandoned. It did indeed reach Bexar to be used in defense of the Alamo. As such, it was pretty possibly melted down following the battle.

Another theory as to the fate of the cannon is less likely but is somewhat more romantic. It says that years later, in 1852, Texas politician Samuel Maverick, who fought in the siege of Bexar and was one of the signers of the Texas Declaration of Independence, was having a house built in the San Antonio area relatively close to the Alamo Plaza. While construction was underway, thirteen of the Alamo cannons were unearthed. They deduced that the cannons had been buried there by Mexicans, retreating after the Battle of San Jacinto. The Mavericks donated most of these cannons to the Alamo Mission, and the cannons remain there on display – and that the cannon was one of these.

In 1874, then-widowed Mary Maverick had the cannon sent to New York. The bronze cannon was melted down and recast as a church bell before it came back home. That version of the story claims that today, the cannon hangs in the church's belfry that the Mavericks helped fund: St. Mark's Episcopal Church in San Antonio.

The debate surrounding the fate of the cannon only reaffirms its importance in history.

The Provisional Government Crumbles

Now that they believed they had sent Mexico running, the problem facing the Volunteer Army of the People of Texas was boredom. Many of the Texian volunteers returned to their nearby homes for the Christmas holiday. Yet, hundreds of American volunteers had crossed into Texas to assist in the Siege at Bexar. Now, these men remained in Texas, far from their homes and families, with nothing to occupy their time. Somehow, this group, along with any Texians who were still itching for a fight, focused on the idea of taking the town of Matamoros.

Indeed, taking Matamoros would be a tremendous victory. This prosperous port town linked Mexico with the rest of the world. Whoever controlled it would have a distinct strategic advantage. A flurry of planning went through San Felipe de Austin as officials gathered to bicker over the strategy of taking the town, but the goal was literally out of reach. Matamoros was far to the south, and there was no feasible way to keep troops supplied with the basics of living on such a long journey. Keeping troops equipped for the Siege of Bexar had been quite tricky enough.

No expeditions or conquests ever literally set out for Matamoros. However, this battle-that-never-was had a disastrous outcome, as if it was the first domino to fall in a long succession of missteps. One would-be commander, eager to ready himself for a battle in Matamoros, took supplies from Bexar without the provisional government's permission.

This "borrowing" of supplies made provisional Governor Smith paranoid. He believed that the interim council had conducted secret machinations behind his back. In a fury, he fired them all.

"Not so fast," said the council, refusing to accept his authority. Two days later, in their "Proclamation of the People of Texas," they impeached Smith. Their proclamation put Lieutenant Governor James W. Robinson in charge, technically. Still, Governor Smith refused to relinquish leadership or the archives. In his mind, he was still the governor and still had the governor's powers. The council kept on meeting as well. So for several weeks, the provisional government of Texas stood divided. No one had full authority to make decisions.

Nevertheless, ordinary Texians felt invigorated by their retaking of San Antonio de Bexar. For the most part, the ordinary person looked forward to an important gathering scheduled on March 1, 1836, in Washington on the Brazos. There, the new, "real" Texas government would be formed. Texians were uninterested in the ongoing squabbling among the members of the provisionary government. But squabbling they were, and this failure to establish firm leadership would come back to haunt them in the weeks ahead.

A Daring Rescue

John Jackson Tumlinson, Jr. and his company of Texas Rangers did not linger around Bexar with the restless leftovers. John Jackson, Jr. went first to Bastrop, north of Gonzales and roughly the same distance from San Antonio as Gonzales was. In Bastrop, John Jackson, Jr. filled out the ranks of his Ranger squad. It was there that young Noah Smithwick signed on, and it is through Noah Smithwick's later historical accounts that we know the details of this harrowing adventure.

The Rangers were at work in Williamson County, protecting the citizens there. One of their assignments was to build the Tumlinson Blockhouse along the Brushy Creek, which would be the first Anglo post in the county. Rangers were accustomed to living "rough," so they camped on the land while they constructed the blockhouse.

On a cold January night in 1836, the Ranger Company of John Jackson, Jr. relaxed around the campfire and prepared their evening meal when an appalling sight appeared before them. A young woman stumbled out of the trees, covered in blood from cuts, scrapes, and scratches, nearly frozen through from the cold and delirious with grief and exhaustion. From what they could gather, she had been wandering for some time through the wild, winter country of Texas entirely alone, with only the ragged clothes on her back. They discovered her name was Sarah Hibbins.

When at last she was coherent enough to speak, Sarah told a terrible tale. Traveling toward their home on the Guadalupe River, her entire family – her brother, her husband, and their two children had been attacked by Comanche natives. Her husband and brother were killed outright, and their possessions plundered. Sarah and the children, an infant and her three-year-old son were taken captive. The baby's crying irritated their Comanche captors, so they murdered the child before its mother's eyes by smashing its head against a tree.

On their return journey to the Comancheria, the Comanche stopped for the night well inside Anglo territory to take shelter from the cold. They were secure in their belief that they would be far away from the territory before anyone discovered their attack. The Comanche left Sarah unbound. They supposed that she would never leave her only remaining child behind, and the child was well-guarded.

However, Sarah knew that the only way to save herself or her son was to try to run for help. After ensuring that her son was tucked under a warm buffalo hide, she slipped away under cover of darkness and then made her way through the countryside. She thought her best hope of finding assistance was to follow the Colorado River south and often trudged through the icy January waters to hide her tracks. In 24 hours, she had traveled about ten miles and finally followed a herd of dairy cows as they wandered their way home toward a nearby Texian settlement. It was by pure luck that she stumbled across the Ranger Company.

Sarah begged the Rangers to save her child. John Jackson, Jr. spared no time in organizing his men to do just that. Luckily, Sarah was able to provide some direction as to the Comanche party's campsite. They set off to find the Comanche campground with the help of their guide. They found the camp at Walnut Creek, near the same place as Sarah had described. The Comanche had likely not moved onward at all that day but instead spent the daylight hours looking for their escaped prisoner. The Rangers' surprise arrival left the Comanche at a disadvantage; they had no time to get to their horses and could only grab a few weapons as they ran for cover in the cedar trees.

Noah Smithwick, himself, shot a Comanche in self-defense, hitting the warrior – though not fatally. While playing dead, the Comanche reloaded his gun and aimed at John Jackson, Jr. Even injured, the downed Comanche shot well enough to kill the captain's horse. Another Ranger took down the Comanche before he could fire on John Jackson, Jr. again.

The Hibbins boy suffered a precarious ordeal. He was well-concealed, wrapped in a blanket on the back of a Comanche mule. When the noise of the fighting caused the mule to start in fear, one Ranger assumed it was a Comanche trying to escape. The Ranger took two shots at the boy, misfiring both times. His third shot came perilously close to striking the boy but was fortunately off-aim because another Ranger recognized the mistake being made and pushed the gun aside at the last moment.

Only one Comanche died during the rescue – the one who had fired on both Smithwick and John Jackson, Jr. The others scrambled away into the brush, were chasing them down would have been impossible. The Rangers accomplished the mission's most important goal: the rescue and retrieval of Sarah Hibbins's only remaining child. They took the little boy with them and returned to the site of the Tumlinson Blockhouse. Sarah, who had suffered such a brutal and terrible ordeal, was emotionally overwhelmed by the miracle of having her son returned. Smithwick's recounting of the happy reunion said few dry eyes at the celebration that night, not even among those toughened Rangers.

As for the Tumlinson Blockhouse, it was successfully built but only in use for a few weeks. By late February, when it was confirmed that Santa Anna and the Centralist Army were setting upon the Alamo, Commander "Three-Legged Willie" Williamson ordered John Jackson, Jr.'s Rangers to return Bastrop.

Native tribe members later razed the Tumlinson Blockhouse. Today, its location is marked with a memorial stone in beautiful Cedar Park of the Block House Creek subdivision of Leander, Texas. Block House Creek is also the location of Tumlinson Park, the Tumlinson Pool, and various other historical markers celebrating the Tumlinson family's service and sacrifices to the State of Texas and its Rangers.

Chapter Five:

Bloody Revolution

Santa Anna Comes to Texas

Texians learned soon enough that their victory at San Antonio de Bexar would not be ignored. The Mexican Army was on its way, under the command of President Santa Anna.

Preparations for the arrival of this sinister force centered around the fortification of the Alamo Mission on the outskirts of San Antonio. Colonel James C. Neill was in command; his extensive knowledge of artillery permitted him to take the little mission's twenty-gun battery and fortify it surprisingly well. Neill believed that the Alamo was the first line of defense against Santa Anna. However, the Alamo and San Antonio themselves were desperately in need of volunteers and supplies. Readers will recall that many of San Antonio's stores had been "requisitioned" away for a raid on Matamoros—which had never happened. Colonel Neill corresponded with Sam Houston, vehemently hoping that supplies could be routed to his fort.

With the dissolution of the provisional government (or with the establishment of two provisional semi-government), Sam Houston remained the uncertain commander of a virtually nonexistent military. This "Army" was no more than a gathering of voluntary Texian recruits and whatever volunteers they could get from the United States. With such limited resources, Houston was undecided whether a garrison at San Antonio was even worth keeping. To determine the fort's usefulness, he sent James Bowie and a company of volunteers to survey the happenings at the Alamo.

Bowie arrived at the Alamo with his troops on January 17 of 1836. Here, he was enamored, as many people would be, by the fiery charisma of Colonel Neill.

Neill gave a passionate argument of the Alamo's defensive importance, convincing Bowie of the truth of the matter. Converted to the cause, Bowie requested the much-needed supplies from Governor Smith. Volunteers began to filter slowly over the next few weeks. These included Colonel William B. Travis and his cavalry, who acted as outriders to warn the Alamo of any impending attacks. On February 8, American politician and celebrity David Crockett arrived with a group of American volunteers.

A misjudgment in timing became the severe first miscalculation made in the Alamo's defense. In early

February, reports came to Colonel Neill that Santa Anna and his army had crossed the Rio Grande and entered Texas. Still, Neill was confident that Santa Anna could not reach the Alamo before March 15.

Thus, the colonel felt no qualms about taking furlough for a family emergency on February 14, leaving Colonel Travis in charge. Neill expected to return in twenty days, well ahead of the enemy's approach. If the timeline had played out the way Neill expected, more reinforcements would have arrived from the newly formed government (for Sam Houston would eventually be sent to help), and Neill would have been present for the battle he had so carefully planned.

The hard fact was that Santa Anna and his massive Centralist army arrived outside San Antonio by February 23, 1836. San Antonio and the Alamo were far from ready to handle the attack. The town was indefensible, so residents fled town or hurriedly took refuge inside the Alamo's walls. The little fortress barricaded itself closed.

On the day of his arrival, Santa Anna demanded the Alamo's surrender. Colonel Travis's unyielding response was to fire a cannon at the Centralist Army. With that, the Centralists began their barrage of cannon fire at the

Alamo's sturdy walls in a siege that would go on for thirteen days.

Texas Rangers Come When Called

When the Siege of the Alamo commenced, Colonel Travis sent a rousing letter to the provisional government, vowing nothing less than "victory or death." He told the provisional leaders that he believed the Alamo could be held until reinforcements arrived.

Unfortunately, reinforcements were minimal – few came, and fewer still were able to make it past the defenses Santa Anna had set up. Santa Anna's army surrounded the Alamo, paying particular attention to passages through which soldiers and communications might ride. Mexican troops posted along the routes had orders to kill, for Santa Anna gave the command that no quarter would be given to enemy forces. To him, "enemy forces" included civilians and surrendered soldiers.

During the grimmest moments of the Alamo's siege, a group of 32 men from Gonzales managed to fight through the Mexican troops to reinforce the beleaguered

Alamo soldiers. Captain Albert Martin led the group, including an estimated fourteen Texas Rangers under the separate command of Second Lieutenant Kimball. One member of the reinforcements was James Tumlinson, Jr.'s son, George Tumlinson, of the Gonzales Ranging Company of Mounted Volunteers, and he, like all the others, would fight to his death in defense of the Alamo.

Captain John Jackson Tumlinson, Jr.'s Rangers operated in Bastrop and Gonzales from about February 28, under orders to continue protecting the upper portion of the frontier and conducting spy patrols in the direction of San Antonio, according to the recollections of Noah Smithwick. From Bastrop, they also aided and accompanied those who took supplies to Gonzales. The irony of this tragic situation is that while Captain Tumlinson's men were stationed in Bastrop, awaiting orders from Major Williamson, the provisional government in San Felipe recommended to Williamson that Tumlinson's Rangers should proceed at once to San Antonio de Bexar to aid the Texians. Whether countermanded or lost in transport, these orders never reached Captain Tumlinson.

However, additional and systematic research by Thomas Rick Lindley suggests that Captain Tumlinson's group did far more than merely provide aid to those who gathered nearby. According to Lindley, another group of both volunteers and Rangers, about fifty men from Goliad and others from Gonzalez, managed to slip past the Mexican Army to aid the defenders of the Alamo, arriving before daylight on the morning of March 4, 1836. His research indicates that a number of these Rangers were members of Captain Tumlinson's company. In part, Lindley's thorough investigation into the Alamo's siege caused a significant stir among Alamo scholars because he called into question the considerable reliance that had been placed on the accounts of Noah Smithwick. Smithwick's literature is remarkable. However, it did rely on the memories of nonagenarians, which easily could be argued as fallible.

The problem with confirming or denying the theories of the Alamo's brave defense is that in the chaos of the siege and the subsequent massacre, any records of defenders entering the fortress following March 3 are uncertain. Due to proximity and the constantly changing ranks of the various groups as men volunteered for service, it is quite possible that members of Captain Tumlinson's group did join in with those who broke through the Mexican blockade to aid the besieged Alamo.

Other volunteers, including Ranger companies, made serious attempts to reach the Alamo to assist. Still, Santa Anna's blockade almost always proved too dangerous to cross. Even the furloughed Colonel Neill had raised a relief force of about 300 men at the ready in Gonzales but could never return to his fortress in time to help. Even Colonel Fannin, who had gathered a considerable force in Goliad, did not come to the Alamo's aid. Some accounts say his officers refused to comply, while others blame Fannin specifically for calling off the mission.

Even aside from those who managed to make it to the Alamo in time to participate in the final battle, the Texas Rangers, who had some form of authority established, at least seemed able to provide support or assistance to the Alamo's defenses. Authority was precisely what the provisional government lacked and why it ultimately failed the Alamo defenders as they suffered under Santa Anna's attack.

No Reinforcements from the Provisional Government

Behind the battered Alamo walls, James Bowie had fallen deathly ill on the second day of the siege with an illness they called "typhoid pneumonia." The Alamo was under the siege of cannon fire for days, with the troops doing what they could to shore up the walls at night with whatever materials they could find. Colonel Travis, unable to comprehend why their government had abandoned them, lost hope for rescue or reinforcements.

In Washington on the Brazos, delegates gathered to declare Texas's independence, form a new constitution, and elect officials. Beyond that, they had no resources to give in service to the Alamo. General Santa Anna's early arrival meant that they were already too late to send any significant help. Sam Houston tried, in vain, to confirm his authority to take action, but since no actual government functioned yet, no one was able to grant him the power to act.

The delegation's foregone conclusion of declaring independence was seemingly an abrupt switch from the attitude of four months earlier when the Volunteer Army of the People of Texas had marched on San Antonio de Bexar. After winning San Antonio de Bexar, Texians thought themselves invincible. Now, they were scrambling for assistance.

At that time, they claimed to be fighting in support of Federalism and the Mexican Constitution of 1824. Now, independence for Texas was the only choice.

What factors had changed their minds, from cockiness to fear, from federalism to independence?
The Texians' taking of San Antonio had driven an occupying Mexican general out of the region. But General Santa Anna's swift arrival and his fearsome reputation certainly caused enough for fear. The Alamo is considered the first line of defense, was, to the dismay of Texians, likely their last line of security as well, unless circumstances dramatically changed. A spirited group of volunteers surely could not be enough to defeat the monster at their doorstep.

Ultimately, the push for a declaration of independence was a financial one, pressured by the United States. Texians were rich in land but relatively poor in actual money, so they had few resources to outfit the army they badly needed. What's more, they didn't have nearly enough people to form an army that could rival the size of Santa Anna's.

Stephen Austin and other Texas agents were busily drumming up volunteer support in the United States and trying to secure bank loans. Southern banks were interested in supporting Texas, but *only* if it was independent of Mexico.

The logic behind this requirement was the commonly held belief that United States statehood would soon follow for an independent Texas. Texas, where slavery was legal, would break the tie of slave-holding versus non-slave-holding states in the Union. Therefore, to get any helpful support from the United States, independence was suddenly necessary for Texas. Texians were afraid that they couldn't win against Santa Anna without the United States' support. Therefore, independence it would be.

George C. Childress headed the committee to write Texas's Declaration of Independence. The document was written almost overnight. It was dated March 2, 1836, and adopted unanimously without edits or amendments. On March 4, the convention's delegates confirmed that Sam Houston was commander of Texas's military and charged him to usurp the forces and take the fight to Santa Anna. He departed Washington on the Brazos on the evening of March 6 with what troops were available, with the full intent of bringing aid to the Alamo.

Houston did not know that the Alamo had already fallen that very morning. And those who fought, and died, at the Alamo were never aware that they sacrificed their lives for an independent Texas.

The Fall – and Fallout – of the Alamo

Santa Anna's attack on the Alamo was without mercy. He believed, mistakenly, that fear and demoralization would stop the revolution – this troublesome Texian uprising – in its wrongheaded tracks. His ruthlessness extended not only to Texians and any Tejanos fighting alongside them but even to his soldados, the soldiers of the Mexican Centralist Army. His officers could not understand his insistence on attacking the still-standing walls of the Alamo at dawn on March 6 of 1886, nor his willingness to sacrifice shocking numbers of his soldiers in a gambit to climb the fort's walls and gain access.

The cost of taking the Alamo was high even to Santa Anna's troops, yet he ordered the attack without thought to their lives before, during, or after the battle.

At 6:00 a.m., cries of fear woke the exhausted Alamo protectors as the Mexicans, at least 1,700 infantry and 300 cavalries (though some estimates have the number at almost twice as many) advanced on the Alamo's walls. Defenders who managed to grab their guns and race to the ramparts shot down the front-line soldados. Still, more soldados came after them, moving on the walls within the tide of their numbers. When Santa Anna felt the battle was progressing too slowly, he had his reserve troops fire a volley into the fray, killing more Mexicans than Texians. Outside the fortress walls, Santa Anna's lancers were placed strategically on escape routes to cut down anyone who attempted to run from the battle.

The Alamo's Colonel Travis shot his gun twice before he took a fatal bullet in the head. The Alamo's defenders fought as well as they could, but sheer numbers were against them. Once the terrified Centralist soldiers managed to mount the walls and open an inner door, the residents of the Alamo were vastly outnumbered. Mexican soldados flooded into the camp, killing every man they found. They slaughtered Jim Bowie in his sickbed.

Only a final few who had taken refuge inside the Alamo Church saw the end of the battle. David Crocket was reputedly among them. Santa Anna ordered that these remaining prisoners be hacked apart with swords, a final act so unfair that many of Santa Anna's men looked away in shame. Some women and children were spared, but aside from couriers outside the fort at the time of the attack, the only man who survived was a Tejano who managed to convince the soldados he had been a prisoner.

In the aftermath of the battle, General Santa Anna continued to ignore the wellbeing of his troops. He made no provisions for a field hospital. His secretary recorded that over 100 wounded Mexican soldiers died from lack of proper medical care, even though their injuries were not necessarily fatal.

For two days and two nights, a fiendish fire burned outside San Antonio, fed by the corpses drug from inside the Alamo's walls by weary Mexican troops. Likewise, a blaze of vengeance ignited inside the Texians in their outrage and grief at Santa Anna's monstrous act.

Worse still, the uncaring Santa Anna was not finished showing the depths of his brutality.

Runaway Scrape

There was hardly a soul in the town of Gonzales who was unrelated to, or friends with, someone who had fought at the Alamo. When word came that the fort had fallen and almost all inside were slaughtered, the town's grief was terrible. Sam Houston arrived soon after that to receive the news. While the siege of the Alamo had raged on, the Alamo's furloughed Colonel Neill had raised a force of over 300 untrained volunteers in Gonzales, and these men stood ready. Yet, Sam Houston knew that against Santa Anna's army, they did not stand a chance.

On March 13, the now-widowed Susannah Dickinson, the only white Texian woman who had been inside the Alamo, reached Gonzales with her child to tell the full scale of the horrors that had happened there. She brought a message from Santa Anna: any who opposed him would meet the same fate.

Terror spread through the population as fast as word of this threat could travel, and at once, thousands of Texians gathered what possessions they could carry – or no possessions at all, in some cases - and made a mass exodus east. Panic-stricken, they fought their way through the Texas wilderness toward the Sabine River and the presumed safety of the United States. This flight from the Texian colonies became known by a few names: the Runaway Scrape, the Great Runaway, or the Sabine Shoot.

Because so many men had been killed, and a more significant number volunteered to stay and fight, the Runaway Scrape consisted mainly of women fending alone for themselves and their children. The children were often so young that their mothers had to carry them, leaving them helpless to take any additional supplies. March weather worsened the conditions as heavy spring rains began to batter the land, flood the roads, and turn Texas into a muddy bog. River ferries could not handle the numbers of fleeing Texians. Lines of hundreds stood on the shore. Some people elected to swim across or cross on foot, slogging through the deep bottomlands mud.

Tejanos also fled, fearing reprisals if Santa Anna should believe them in league with the Texians. If anything, their flight was even more complicated because they had to cross Texian lands, where they did not speak the language and where prejudice against Mexicans was particularly vicious at the moment.

The number of deaths caused by the Runaway Scrape is unrecorded. Chaos reigned, and there was simply no way to keep track of loss of life. Amid this unrest, however, the Texas Rangers once more proved their value. Some stayed behind to help clear the towns and ensure that colonists could escape, and some accompanied larger bands of colonists to afford some protection to them. John Jackson, Jr.'s Ranger Company was ordered out of Bastrop to aid the colonists. He was able to reunite with his own family and ensure their passage along with that of others. His Ranger duties kept him distant from the following few events in the Texas Revolution. Therefore, he and his men were not available to participate in the deciding Battle of San Jacinto. Even so, with their brave aid to the victims of Santa Anna's fear campaign, they served a desperately needed role in the Texas Revolution.

The Battle of Coleto Creek

Santa Anna was not the only Mexican general leading troops through Texas. While his troops regrouped after the siege of the Alamo, General José de Urrea was on the march along the coastline with the intent to securing port towns in their geographical order: San Patricio, Refugio, Goliad, Victoria, and Brazoria.

Texas's General Fannin had 400 troops in Goliad – he had gathered these in a plan to aid the Alamo, which had never come to fruition. At the time, he was the most significant force of the Texian Army. Urrea took Patricio and Refugio. General Fannin was ordered to retreat from Goliad to avoid the Mexican Army and rendezvous with Sam Houston and his men (including Colonel Neill's 300+ volunteers) at the Colorado River. Fannin led his troops from Goliad on March 19, 1836.

Fannin made an error in judgment, supposing the number of troops under his command would dissuade any attack. He allowed his men to stop for rest on the wide-open and indefensible ground with no access to water. Urrea's troops, however, were in quick pursuit of this Texian division. They came upon them fast and attacked, leaving Fannin's men with no choice but to square up a defense around their broken-down armory wagon as enemies approached from all sides. Without water, Fannin's troops fought through the long night, battling thirst as well as gunfire. In the morning, the Mexicans had reinforcements that included a howitzer.

The rapid-fire gun shredded what remained of the Texian defense.

Fannin had no choice but to surrender. He and the other survivors were taken back to Presidio La Bahia in Goliad and imprisoned there, and General Urrea continued his trek up the coast.

The Goliad Massacre

On March 27, 1836, the prisoners of Presidio La Bahia (numbering somewhere between 425 and 450 Texians) were marched to a mile outside of town. Here, the Mexican soldados halted the prisoners and opened fire, slaughtering all but the 28 who managed to escape to tell the story. The soldados executed the prisoners under the orders of General Santa Anna.

Inside the Presidio, about 40 of Fannin's men, including Fannin himself, had been too injured to join the march or had been purposely held back. These men were, for the most part, murdered on the spot. The Presidio's commander, shocked by Santa Anna's merciless orders, did what he could to spare the lives of men he deemed to have valuable skills, but this saved a minimal number of prisoners. Colonel Fannin was the last to die in the Goliad massacre before a firing squad shot him in the face and threw his body on a pile of others.

If Santa Anna had intended to frighten the Texians into submission, he had managed to fail on two levels. Indeed, the Runaway Scrape sent thousands fleeing east toward the Sabine. Still, the plight of these brave women refugees became another rallying cry for the Texian army, along with the martyrdom of men at the Alamo and the Goliad Massacre. Santa Anna's abominable acts did nothing short of madden the volunteers. The men of Texas were ready to exact vengeance on Mexico with righteous fury.

A Long Road to San Jacinto

The final battle between Santa Anna's forces and the Texian Army would not occur until April 21, nearly an entire month later. In that time, Sam Houston led his men on a long and sometimes confusing journey that leaves historians questioning his thinking. For a man who would soon be considered the "savior of Texas," he seemed for several weeks to be avoiding a confrontation at all costs.

He took his troops from town to town, burning places to the ground behind them, so there would be no spoils for the Mexicans to take. Once the settlers had fled their homes, Houston ordered the burning of Gonzales. He burned Burnam's Ferry on the Colorado River and then marched his men south to Beason's, where they waited in vain for Colonel Fannin to arrive. After news of the Goliad Massacre and Fannin's death, Houston took his men into further retreat toward San Felipe de Austin. Much to the shock and dismay of his troops, who believed that Austin should be protected no matter what, Houston ordered that town burned to the ground as well.

As they traveled, the Texian army picked up new volunteers and lost old ones. Frequently, men who had already aided their families in the Runaway Scrape returned to join the march. Men who wondered if there would ever be a fight and if they had any chance of winning it lost their nerve and abandoned them. But three or four other Tumlinson sons met up with companies or simply arrived to fight unattached, in time for San Jacinto. Though John Jackson, Jr. was busy with Ranger duties elsewhere, his younger brothers, Peter and

Joe Tumlinson were both at San Jacinto. Sons of James Tumlinson, Sr., John, and possibly David, also joined the campaign through Captain Heard's Company. David's presence at San Jacinto is likely, but cannot be confirmed, because he died not long after the battle was won, seemingly from unrelated causes.

The Texian army finally took two weeks of refuge on a plantation owned by a man named Groce. Groce gave his home to the military for a field hospital. The men were able to heal and rest from exposure, illnesses, and injuries. Additionally, Sam Houston arranged for some on-the-spot military training to better prepare these very green volunteers for a fight.

Perhaps the two weeks were much needed and well spent. Nevertheless, Houston's army and government both grew impatient with him. Still, Houston stalled. Even after a strong letter from the ad interim government telling him to take the fight to Santa Anna, Houston led his men across the Brazos River, always moving further and further east and away from Santa Anna.

Historians speculate that there was a method to Houston's strange behavior. He was likely taking his army to the Nacogdoches River to obtain the aid of the

United States. He knew that President Andrew Jackson's orders were for the U.S. Army to intervene if Santa Anna crossed that river. Houston knew that the assistance of the United States would assure their victory. At the same time, Houston feared that his mostly untrained, volunteer army with low numbers and inferior supplies would be devastated by the Mexican soldados. His plan was solid enough; he only failed to consider how violently the Texians wanted revenge for the evils that Santa Anna had done or how desperately they would wish to protect their stake in Texas.

Eventually, they forced Houston's hand: the ad interim government commanded him to engage the enemy or be replaced in no uncertain terms. Houston reluctantly turned the troops south toward Harrisburg. They arrived in time to see the last of Harrisburg burning down.

Battle of San Jacinto

It was then that Houston received a piece of news that turned the numerical odds, for once, in favor of the Texians. Houston's scouts informed him that Santa Anna was camped nearby with a small detachment – only 700 men instead of his usual numbers of twice that many or more. A geographical advantage was in place: for Santa Anna to return to his entire army, he would need to cross the San Jacinto River via Lynch's Ferry. On April 20, Houston brought his army to Lynch's Ferry ahead of any Mexican troops. Later that day, when Santa Anna arrived, he was astonished to find himself facing down a Texian army of superior numbers. He had incorrectly assumed they were still encamped at Groce's plantation.

While Santa Anna's smaller force was camped within only 500 yards of Texians and was pretty hemmed in by water to one side and a forest to another, Houston still hesitated to attack. Up until his army was on the verge of mutiny, Houston seemed to retain the hope of gathering the United States to their side in the fight. But his council of war would have no more of it, especially when waiting around allowed time for the Mexican Army to gather 500 reinforcements, thanks to the arrival of General Cos to Santa Anna's aid.

It must be said that Houston's delay gave the Texians an unforeseen strategic advantage. Santa Anna's men were exhausted from spending the last 24 hours erecting a camp, barricading it, and waiting to fend off the attack they were sure would come during the previous night, or at dawn, or indeed during daylight hours…and General Cos's troops were just as worn down from their fast march to reinforce Santa Anna's men. It seemed so unlikely that the Texians would attack in the late afternoon or early evening. Santa Anna ordered a stand-down, allowing the soldados to collapse into their cots for some rest.

The sun was almost setting on April 21 when the Texian army began to slip across the field between the troops. The Tejanos who fought alongside the Texians wore cardboard signs in their hats to avoid being mistaken for the enemy. Thanks to the tall grass and a topographical depression in the middle of the field, they were able to get well within the musket range of the Mexican camp before anyone realized they had approached. The surprise attack was so effective that the Mexican army was beaten in 18 minutes, with Texian casualties limited to nine deaths and 30 wounded. Infuriated by the events of the Alamo and Goliad, many Texian troops exacted heedless, bloody revenge on even the Mexicans who surrendered.

The Capture of the Great Santa Anna

Amid the chaos, General Santa Anna found the fastest horse he could and escaped. Sam Houston had the forethought to send men to destroy the bridge that Santa Anna, or anyone else, would need to flee the area. The mighty general, unable to forge the swollen river, abandoned his horse and spent the night hiding in the woods. He stripped himself of all insignia so that if captured, he could not be identified.

The following day, Texian troops discovered him hiding in the swamp. The Texians had no idea who they had captured until they noticed other Mexicans treating the man with deference. Once they, at last, deduced whom they had in hand, they took him to Sam Houston. Houston had been seriously injured in the fight, one of his ankles shattered by a gunshot.

When led before Sam Houston, Santa Anna complimented his adversary and was quick to request that he be treated with the mercy that a nobleman such as General Houston would surely grant. No doubt in a great deal of pain, the enraged Houston reminded Santa Anna that such understanding certainly had not been given to Texians at either the Alamo or Goliad. Still, Houston refrained from executing the Mexican general, although his men were more than eager to assist with the task. There were better uses for their captured villain.

The Tumlinson Family in the Texas Revolution

From the time Texians gathered in Gonzales to raise the "COME AND TAKE IT!" flag over the bronze cannon to the final battle at San Jacinto, eight Tumlinson men fought in the Texas Revolution. These included James Tumlinson, Sr. plus four of his sons: Littleton, John, David, and George (who died at the Alamo), and three sons of John Jackson Tumlinson, Sr.: John Jackson, Jr., Peter (who was present at the meeting between Santa Ana and Sam Houston), and Joe. They served in either Ranger Units or the Volunteer Army.

Though San Jacinto's battle essentially ended the revolution, the Tumlinsons' service to Texas was by no means at an end. John Jackson Jr. and his brothers Peter and Joe, as Texas Rangers, turned their full attention to an even greater danger: the increasingly violent threat of the Comanche.

End of the Texas Revolution

Essentially, victory at San Jacinto ended the revolution in Texas, but the outcome was not what Texians had hoped it would be. This is not to say that Texians gave up or gave in; they did neither. Their resilience was remarkable. However, the conditions in the colonies to which they returned were disheartening, and the changes for which they fought were slow to come.

General Houston and the captured Santa Anna agreed. Anger burned bright toward the hated Mexican commander, and Texians made repeated demands for his immediate execution. Houston knew that other Mexican generals were in Texas with impressive numbers of soldados behind them. His concern was that the execution of Santa Anna would bring further retribution. Santa Anna remained wily as always: he agreed to send the Mexican army into retreat in exchange for his life.

On May 14, 1836, the two Treaties of Velasco were signed between General Santa Anna and ad interim President Burnet. The existence of two treaties was purposeful. Briefly, the first treaty was meant to cease hostilities and return Santa Anna to Mexico. Once that was accomplished, the second treaty would go into effect, making Texas independent from Mexico. Unfortunately, neither of the Velasco agreements produced results. Mexico declared that anything Santa Anna signed or agreed to while he was a prisoner was meritless.

In the weeks following the Battle at San Jacinto, Santa Anna remained in the custody of the Texian government, his life in constant danger. Anyone who had a friend or relative die at the Alamo or in Goliad was eager to string up the general.

At a discreet distance, Texian troops led by Thomas Jefferson Rusk followed behind the Mexican Centralist army, ensuring that they retreated to the south of the Rio Grande, as promised.

The Spirit of Texas

Spring rains were incredibly violent and profuse that year. Flooding and mud hampered the poor souls in the Runaway Scrape as they fled. Now, as they were assured of the retreat of the Mexican Army, these same folks made their way back home through even worse conditions. Storm winds produced high waves on the seas. Flooding caused bogs of deadly quicksand. Alligators made out far better than humans in the new swampy landscape. More than a few Texians lost their lives to the lurking reptiles. One "silver lining" was that the Mexican Army fared no better, so exhausted and depleted that they had no energy to stage any rebellion in their struggles to retreat.

Having lost everything in the Runaway Scrape, Texians returned to find their homes sacked and towns burned down. Their losses were incalculable, for not only had their homes, towns, and everything for which they had struggled for fifteen years been swept away, but most of them had lost friends and family in the tide of death that came with this incredible year. There had been battles and massacres, the unpredictable elements, and the deprivations of war.

Despite these dire conditions, Texians were made of specific hardy stock and were unwilling to quit. With remarkable fortitude, they picked up and started again, regrouping families, forming new families, building or rebuilding, and stubbornly attaching themselves to a land that they now believed they hard-earned in spirit, as well as in hard work. They cleaved themselves to their new "independent" homeland with a strong sense of nationalism. As one proud genealogist of his family's history, Samuel Tumlinson calls this period the end of the age of "Texians" and the birth of "Texans." To this day, Texan pride goes on unwaveringly in the descendants of the Texians who made such sacrifices.

Horse Marines: A Texas Rangers Story

The Texas Rangers played a significant role in the return to normalcy. While the Army was engaged in dealing with the Mexican retreat, Rangers continued to protect those who struggled to return to and rebuild their homes. Native attacks seriously plagued towns such as Bastrop during 1836, and it was only with Ranger intervention that the aggressions were curbed.

General Houston went to New Orleans to recover from his war injury. Secretary of War Thomas Jefferson Rusk took over as temporary Commander of the Army. While he and his troops were quietly "escorting" the Mexican Army south of the Rio Grande, Rusk feared that another Mexican attack might come by sea. In June 1836, Rusk sent Ranger Captain Isaac Watts Burton and 30 more

Texas Rangers to patrol the coastal zone that fell between the Guadalupe River and Mission Bay.

Sure enough, a suspicious schooner called *Watchman* showed up in Copano Bay, with no flag flying. The Rangers never approached a task in quite the same manner as a "regular" army, relying on spycraft, bending the ordinary rules of engagement to get the job done. Captain Burton had his men hide in the forest near the beach. With a bit of acting, two of his men set themselves upon the shore as if they were Mexican soldados in need of help. They signaled wildly to the ship. In response, the boat raised its flags: an unusual combination of both the United States flag and the colors of Texas. Captain Burton was fully aware that no U.S. Naval ship would fly the flags of two countries at once, and he suspected that this was a ruse. He instructed his actors to wave back the Mexican flag, and the ship promptly switched to the Mexican flag as its standard.

This appeared to be an opportunity. The *Watchman* sent out a dinghy of men to pick up the "Mexicans" ashore. Strangely, once they arrived, the Mexican men were nowhere to be found. Sounds from the forest nearby prompted an investigation.

When the dinghy returned to the *Watchman*, it was rowed not by its Mexican soldados, but by Texas Rangers wearing Mexican uniforms. The Rangers boarded the *Watchman* and quite quickly subdued those aboard, throwing them on the brink. The quick-thinking Captain Burton was not finished just yet. He thought that surely, more ships would soon follow. As he predicted, two more Mexican schooners arrived in Copano Bay. The new "captain" of the *Watchman* was polite enough to signal invitations to the other schooners' captains and officers to join him on the *Watchman* for a celebratory dinner. Soon enough, both schooners had the Rangers. Each additional capture added to the windfall for Texas. All three schooners were loaded with supplies and ammunition.

On June 22, all three ships left Copano Bay together and headed for Velasco, under the control of the Texas Rangers. Tales of Captain (soon to be Major) Burton and his "Horse Marines" were told not only in Texas but throughout the United States, another example of the legendary audacity and courage of the Texas Rangers.

Chapter Six:

Comanche War

Threat from the North

Just when it seemed that hostilities with Mexico had moved into the stage of bloodless but fruitless negotiations, a new threat emerged. Relations between colonists and the Comanche were never good, but until 1836, threats from several closer tribes had been the primary focus of the colonists' fears and the Texas Rangers' wrath.

It hardly escaped the notice of the Native tribes when the Mexicans and Texians went to war; this opened an opportunity for the Natives to step in, raiding and looting places abandoned during the Runaway Scrape.

The Comanche, too, took advantage of the disruption in the Texian colonies. Their opening salvo was the attack of Parker's Fort (sometimes called the Fort Parker massacre), a secluded religious sect of Texians who did not take part in the revolution.

The residents of Parker's Fort had taken care to establish a secure fortress with 12-foot walls and two blockhouses and make peaceful arrangements with the surrounding tribes. For a couple of years, Elder Parker and his descendants worked and worshiped quietly there.

The Parkers permitted the Texas Rangers access to and used the fort; it is theorized that the Parkers were not aware of the intense hatred and mistrust between Native tribes and the Rangers or how the Natives could misconstrue their hospitality toward the Rangers as an aggressive act.

On May 19, 1936, a raiding party of Natives comprised of Kiowas, Caddos, Wichitas, and Comanches approached the fortress under the guise of a white truce flag. They killed five men, raped and maimed at least two women, and took two women and three children captive. The Parkers who survived mainly were those who had escaped into the surrounding forest before the attack or who had been in the fields tending crops at the time. It was many years before the captured were ransomed and returned to their homes.

The attack on Parker's Fort was so brutal and violent that it sent a surge of horror through the Texas people and launched the violent race war between Texans and Comanches, which would not end for decades. The Texas Rangers always stood as the first line of defense.

Penniless

While General Houston recuperated in New Orleans, things changed on the Texas landscape. First, a massive influx of settlers poured over the Sabine River, having decided that Mexico was no longer a threat and that Texas would soon be part of the United States. These new settlers were not "Texian" and had no loyalty to the vision of Stephen Austin, so at once, there was tension between the "Old Texian" elite and these new settlers.

When establishing an interim government, Texas declared its independence but did not set up any way to tax its citizens, so there was no money incoming. Ad interim President Burnet could see the writing on the wall and declared that there must quickly be an actual election. He sent out a proclamation that Texas would hold an election on the first Monday in September of

1836. On the ballot were nominees for President and a straw poll on whether Texas should request statehood with the United States.

Meanwhile, the Texas Army swelled with volunteers from America, who were looking for the excitement of a war with Mexico. Hundreds of men appeared to sign up for service, and at first, Texas was glad to have the increased numbers in case the Mexicans launched another attack. As the weeks passed, however, the new soldiers suffered disappointment when it seemed there was no more fighting to be done.

The major problem was that Texas had no money to pay its officials or soldiers, and this, of course, did not improve the chances that soldiers would obey their commanding officers. The soldiers were known to ransack civilian provisions so often that the Texas Army soon became as feared as the Mexican Army. Eventually, Texas's impoverished government was forced to furlough most of these soldiers, leaving only a standing army of about 600. Rather than return home, most furloughed men remained in Texas and caused trouble – though just as often, these foolhardy newcomers were swindled by sophisticated con artists.

President Sam Houston

Stephen Austin, a year before, would have been the obvious choice for president. Though it was an unfair assessment, many Texan citizens felt that Austin had "abandoned" them by being in the United States during the Revolution, and his popularity was significantly damaged. Meanwhile, among the new citizenry, he was relatively unknown. Other presidential nominees were Henry Smith (remembered for doing a poor job as governor) and Branch T. Archer (who did not want to be president anyway). Eleven days before the election, Sam Houston returned from New Orleans to put his name on the ballot. He won by a landslide of 77 percent of the votes; whereas, Smith got 13 percent and Austin only 10 percent.

Stephen Austin was wounded by the people's loss of faith in him, but he was a practical and gentile man who always worked toward the best possible end for Texas. He was resolute in his goal to make Texas part of the United States. President Houston offered him the position of Secretary of State, which Austin accepted, despite his severely diminished health. Austin eventually planned for Santa Anna to be sent to the relative safety of Washington, DC until he could be shipped back to Mexico City.

As for the annexation vote, 3,277 votes favored joining the United States, with only 91 votes opposed.

Jilted

As the turbulent year of 1836 ended, "independent" Texas found itself in a strange position. Its sovereign status failed to be recognized by either country that mattered: Mexico, which deemed Texas to be a Mexican state still regardless of whatever revolution had occurred or what the imprisoned Santa Anna might have agreed to, and the United States, which was not willing to accept Texas as a new state.

Texas was not yet an appealing acquisition for the United States. President Andrew Jackson and the American Congress decided on December 21, 1836, that Texas could only be considered for statehood if it could maintain its independence from Mexico, a status that was in doubt. Even with the influx of settlers, the Anglo population of Texas was relatively small, certainly not reaching the numbers typical of an American or Mexican state. Texas was also deeply in debt, with no viable method of repayment yet available. Lastly, the United States under Jackson was unwilling to go to war with Mexico over national boundaries. The following year, when Martin Van Buren took the office of United States President, he expressed even less interest in Texas joining the Union.

Probably to save face, the stubborn Texas government "withdrew" its application for inclusion in the United States and continued to function as its own country, despite Mexico's continued insistence that it was no such thing.

The Texas Constitution declared that its presidents could serve only two-year terms and that terms could not be consecutive. When Sam Houston's first term ended in 1838, Mirabeau B. Lamar, formerly vice president, was elected to the presidency. As the second Texan President, Lamar had no interest in statehood anyway, predicting that Texas would become a far greater country than the United States.

Austin

The seat of the Texas government slipped from town to town as it tried to find its footing, and Stephen Austin followed, his already precarious health grinding down with each move. Often, accommodations for government officials were scant and rudimentary. Living in an unheated shack, Austin contracted pneumonia and was too weak to withstand another severe illness. The relatively young founding father died on December 27 of 1836.

For a brief time, Texas's capital was the fledgling township of Houston, obviously named after the Savior of Texas. The land upon which the town settled was of seriously dubious quality, however. The place was hardly more than a swamp, plagued by mosquitos, with no considerations made for sanitation. Diseases such as yellow fever were rampant through the unsteady population. Gigantic rats boldly invaded homes at night and were not afraid to make a meal out of an exposed toe or nose. Though Texas's elected officials were present in the town, rowdy furloughed soldiers comprised a significant portion of the population. In very little time, the town became riddled with saloons, bordellos, and all manner of criminal activity, pickpocketing, swindling, and so on. Everyone was armed, so disputes always ended in bloodshed.

In 1839, the Texas government officials under President Lamar could no longer bear the hardships in Houston, and they moved north to Waterloo on the Colorado River. The town of Houston survived without them, eventually overcoming the difficulties of lawlessness and environment to become a thriving mercantile center that would eventually grow into the great metropolis it is today.

President Lamar was known to dislike and disagree with Sam Houston intensely, so his feelings likely had some influence in relocating the capital. Waterloo was renamed "Austin" – for San Felipe de Austin had been burned to the ground in the Revolution - and at last, a permanent capital was established in honor of the much-revered original Texian.

President Lamar and Comanche Aggression

While he was president, Sam Houston attempted to keep pace with the Native tribes in the area, including the Comanche. Under his administration, Texas Rangers' duties were to police renegade or raiding Natives but not to harass or otherwise harm peaceful tribes. Noah Smithwick, who had recently been a Texas Ranger under the command of John Jackson Tumlinson, Jr., had even spent some time living among the Comanche to learn their ways and had worked with President Houston to try mending the troubles that fueled the Fort Parker massacre. Houston and Smithwick were both friendly with many Native chiefs.

President Lamar had no such sentiments. Lamar had already led troops in intimidation and violence against Native tribes, and he was now determined to drive the Cherokee out of Texas. When tribal leaders asked him for the chance to complete their last harvest before peacefully leaving their lands, he refused to allow them that luxury. In July of 1839, at the Battle of Neches, 500 Texian militiamen attacked over 800 Cherokee and Delaware natives (at least half of non-combatants, women, and children). The natives were ill-prepared for the brutal attack; they had only a couple dozen guns among them for defense.

Nevertheless, President Lamar boasted about the aggressions to Houston, referencing particularly the death of Chief Di'wali, a man whom Houston had considered a friend and ally – and who had been part of ongoing peace negotiations with the Comanche. President Lamar's campaign flew in the face of all attempts at compromise.

A severe but unexpected side effect emerged from the movement of the Texan capital city: the newly named Austin was much closer to the Comancheria, an infringement that the Comanche did not take lightly.

Thanks to the violent actions of President Lamar and the relocation of Austin, which the Comanche saw as an encroachment on their land, anger between the Comanche Natives and Texas increased uncontrollably. Leaders decided there must be a summit to attempt negotiations. The disastrous outcome of this meeting would bring the Texas Rangers into the forefront of protecting the citizens who, as always, were caught in the middle of hostilities.

One More Try for a Treaty

With President Lamar's policies on one side and the anger of the Natives on the other, conflict was almost constant between the Texan settlers and the Comanche and other tribes. It took on a distinctly underhanded flavor, with Mexicans urging the Comanche to cause trouble for the Texans, supplying the Natives with arms and ammunition. The Mexicans knew that the Comanche were now the greatest motivation for the Texans settlers to either leave the land or surrender to Mexico's protection. Likewise, the Comanche were by no means friendly with all other native tribes, and sometimes tribes such as the Lipan would offer to join the Texans in raids against Comanche camps.

Despite President Lamar's actions (or perhaps because of them), both the Texan settlers and the Comanche were willing to try once more for peaceful agreement between their people. San Antonio officials and the Comanche agreed that a summit occurred at the Council House in San Antonio on March 19, 1840. Under an agreed truce, the Comanche were to bring all their Anglo and Mexican hostages to the meeting. In exchange for the return of the hostages, the Texans would recognize the boundaries of the Comancheria.

The Council House Fight

The Comanche arrived as scheduled, with twelve of their chiefs in attendance. As this was meant to be a peaceful exchange, they brought their women and children along. The women and children waited outside on the San Antonio street while the chiefs entered the Council House with their prisoners to begin the negotiations.

Though the Comanche had several hostages with them, only one of them was white: 16-year-old Matilda Lockhart, the captured daughter of a Texan Colonel, who had been held prisoner for well over a year. Her captors had burned, disfigured, and raped the girl throughout her captivity. This alone was cause for an upset. Moreover, when questioned by the San Antonio officials, Matilda reported that she knew of at least fifteen other white prisoners held by Comanche tribes; none of those fifteen had been brought along to the Council House. Comanche spokesperson Chief Maguara excused this by saying that he and the other chiefs had brought their hostages; there was nothing they could do regarding the hostages of other Comanche groups (and there were many; the Comanche nation was not a united one).

Texas militiamen began to gather in the room as the Comanche was informed that, unless they could produce the remaining captives immediately, the chiefs would be held hostage there until those hostages were delivered. The translator had this message and then ascertained how poorly the Comanche would receive this news and quickly excused himself from the room.

The Comanche were naturally unwilling to remain a prisoner, and at once, a fight broke out with the Comanche determined to break their way free of the Council House using their knives and arrows. The Texan militiamen opened fire and, in those close quarters, managed to shoot both Comanche and Texan men. Of course, the situation quickly reduced to complete chaos.

When a few Comanche men managed to escape the Council House, the Comanche women and children waiting outside were alerted to the trouble and tried to escape; they too joined in the fight when they could not run. Armed Texan civilians spilled out of their homes, shooting indiscriminately at any Comanche regardless of age or sex, later using the excuse that all Comanche looked the same to them. While seven Texans died and ten were wounded, the casualties for the Comanche party were far grimmer. Of the 65 Comanche in attendance, 35 were killed, including three women and two children, 29 were taken prisoner (27 women and two elderly men), and one managed to escape the town, mistaken for a Mexican.

The remaining Comanche prisoners were held there. The San Antonio officials intended to exchange the Comanche hostages for the remaining white prisoners held by the Comanches. However, the Texans did not understand the degree to which they had insulted the Comanche and violated their customs. The Comanche had come to the Council House under the flag of truce, and that truce had been inviolately broken – this was unthinkably offensive behavior; their response to the Texan demands was to torture thirteen of the remaining hostages to death. Two of the hostages were allowed to return, probably only to deliver this news.

The Comanche captives eventually were moved out of San Antonio and put to work. There seemed to be little motivation to keep these captives rounded up; all of them were ultimately able to escape to return to their people.

The Comanche nation regrouped in the north and planned their retribution against the Texans who had so cavalierly broken a sacred Native tradition.

Comanche Vengeance

The organization of their revenge in the Comancheria took many months. Twelve Comanche chiefs were killed in the Council House Fight, so mourning and then reorganizing the tribal structure was necessary, and planning for the large-scale raid happened slowly. The Comanche tribes met and decided on one chief to lead the invasion, Buffalo Hump, who had wisely (in retrospect) declined to attend the Council House Summit.

It was not until August of 1840 that the Comanche raid began, the most significant Native force to ever assemble against the settlers of Texas. Buffalo Hump summoned together all bands of Comanches to join the attack. The raiding party consisted of approximately 400 Comanche warriors. Once more, their women and children traveled with them, so a group of over 1000 Comanche, along with their pack animals, some of their Kiowa allies, and many Mexican guides, descended upon Texas, moving south, make its way across territory that, previously, had been considered safe for white settlers. They moved profoundly and quickly into the colonial areas, south of Gonzales, in a pillaging sweep that would take them across the Guadalupe Valley.

A traveling postal carrier saw them near Gonzales and warned the town of the raid's movements, but Gonzales was not a target for the Comanche. They were moving toward Victoria and the coast. As it happened, since 1839, John Jackson Tumlinson, Jr. was commissioned by the Texan Congress to captain a squad of Rangers, called the Tumlinson Spy Company, and protect the settlement of Gonzales. Once made aware of the Comanche invasion, John Jackson Jr. gathered his Rangers and took off to pursue the war party.

The Comanche Raid approached Victoria on August 6; the unwarned citizens assumed they were a friendly tribe; by the time the raiding party was upon them, it was too late to protect themselves. The Comanche killed 15 citizens of Victoria and took over 1500 horses – a tremendous prize for the raid but a terrible burden to the raid's travel speed. They moved next toward Linville.

By this time, three separate Ranger companies were on the Comanche trail, and as they met up, they joined together. Because of John Jackson Jr's seniority, he was given command of all three Ranger companies. They moved along the trail of burning and pillaging left behind by the Comanche but could not seem to gain on the massive group, always about twenty miles behind. The Comanche were upon Linnville before anyone could catch up to them.

Linnville was a thriving seaside port for the Texan settlers, and its destruction would cripple the Texas economy while benefitting both Comanche and Mexican interests. At the approach of the enormous raiding party, Linnville citizens took refuge on the ocean, madly rowing themselves out to a schooner anchored in the bay, far enough away to be out of the reach of Comanche arrows. From the boat, the Linnville citizens watched their town looted and destroyed.

The treasure of Linnville was more ornamental than anything, as shipments had recently arrived of hundreds of ladies' hats and parasols, but the Comanche were exultant. They paraded through the Linnville wreckage sporting bright bonnets, waving parasols, and unfurling long bolts of cloth. Meanwhile, they wiped Linnville from existence, destroying every building and even slaughtering what livestock they did not wish to transport so that nothing would remain for the citizens.

Finally finished with the destruction of Linnville and heavily loaded down with their prizes, the brightly adorned raiding party turned northward to start their long march back to the Comancheria. Their pace had slowed to a crawl. Finally, they were moving more slowly than the news of their attacks could travel so that the protectors of Texas could not only catch up but anticipate their path of travel.

The Battle of Plum Creek

On August 12, 1840, soldiers of the Texas Republic, militiamen, and the three gathered squads of Texas Rangers lay in wait at Plum Creek for the Comanches' raiding party. In charge of the militiamen and soldiers was regular army General Felix Huston. Huston was not known for being a crafty tactician, and when the Comanche warriors on horseback approached, he had his men assume old-school ground-based tactics, square formations from which his soldiers must stand still and shoot.

Comanche warriors were far too agile and versatile on horseback, and their sweeps past the grounded men meant they were moving targets against stationary ones. The odds were heavily in their favor; each sweep with their horsemen meant dead Texas militia. The Texas Rangers, on the other hand, being on horseback, were able to interfere with the Comanche line. Ranger captains pleaded for General Huston to let his men take to horseback, seeing the unprotected men on the ground. Huston refused and kept his men in their nearly useless defensive position.

Suddenly the Comanche were in disarray as one of their mighty chiefs fell. Ranger captains quickly spotted the opportunity and pointed it out to General Huston, shouting that the Comanche were "whipped" and demoralized and that now was the time to strike, if only the General would allow his men the advantage of their horses. But still, General Huston refused.

Having had enough of the General's stubbornness, and before the Comanche could regain their advantage, the horse-riding Rangers charged at the Comanche, beckoning the militia captains to do the same. At this point, the chain of command broke down. Rangers were armed with single-shot flintlock pistols, so they had to make every shot count. They wouldn't dare try shooting until they were close enough to be confident of a hit. Their charge terrified the 1500 captured horses and started a thunderous stampede, raising so much dust that the Comanche could not see. The confused Natives scattered, abandoning their stolen horses and escaping the battlefield, but killing most of their captives in the process. They left behind the ponderous loot they had stolen and fled. The Texas Rangers pursued them for fifteen miles but were unable to catch up. At sunset, the Rangers returned to the site of the battle to find the militiamen sorting through the incredible trove of goods left behind.

In the aftermath of the battle, General Huston tried to take credit for the victory. Yet the truth was widely acknowledged: had the Ranger captains not taken charge of the fight, the Texas forces would have been picked off by the Comanche a little at a time.

Though the Comanche would continue to attack isolated homesteads in northern Texas, they never again went so far south into Texas or attacked in such large numbers.

A Revolver to the Rescue

While it was confirmed that the Battle of Plum Creek ensured that Comanche raiders were ever again leery of venturing far into Texas, it was by no means their last raid or the last encounter that Texas Rangers would have with the tribe. Having witnessed the fight at Plum Creek, Ranger Captains realized the definite disadvantages suffered by the Rangers (and other Texas militia) against these horsemen from the Comancheria. The Comanche were elegant and expert horse riders. The Rangers acknowledged that they needed to learn Comanche styles of horseback riding, using the horse's body as a shield, and imitate the Comanche methods of ground stealth to fight them successfully.

The Comanche also were armed with bows and arrows, at which their skill was equally masterful. The Rangers were armed with Kentucky Rifles. While famous for their accuracy, Kentucky Rifles required a deadly amount of time to reload. A Comanche could shoot up to twelve arrows in the time it took a Ranger to load, fire, then reload his gun, and, what's more, a Ranger was forced to dismount to reload that gun, leaving himself vulnerable on the ground for several crucial seconds.

The invention of the Colt-Paterson five-shot revolver in 1837 was the solution – it was the first commercially available repeating firearm that used a revolving cylinder. Ranger captains requisitioned enough of the pistols to outfit the Rangers, finally allowing them the advantage of remaining on horseback long enough to fire five rounds off – and the Rangers were well-known as deadly shots. The Comanche lost their last advantage against the Texas Rangers.

Chapter Seven:

The Proud State of Texas

Annexation at Last

Following Lamar's presidency, Sam Houston was elected once more and served another two years. During this time, he rigorously sought statehood. Then, in 1844, Texas elected Anson Jones as its fourth and last President. Jones had served as Sam Houston's Secretary of State during Houston's second term. Jones picked up where Houston had left off, continuing the eager correspondence with annexation advocates in the United States.

In the United States, the paradigm of Manifest Destiny had taken hold and was highly influential in the 1844 Presidential election. Should the United States admit Texas, the government in Mexico made it clear that they would declare war. James K. Polk was the only presidential candidate willing to support Texas annexation even at the risk of war with Mexico. Since his philosophy was well-matched to the feelings of the United States' citizens, Polk won the election by a large margin.

John Tyler, the sitting United States President, moved fast. Since Texas seemed destined to become a state, he wanted to make it happen during his final weeks in office. President-Elect Polk agreed; he did not care who took the credit for Texas's annexation as long as it happened.

Efforts thus far to admit Texas to the United States had been unsuccessful because of the abolitionist vote in the Senate. Northern states did not want another slave-holding state in the Union. Therefore, Tyler decided to achieve Admission by Joint Resolution of Congress, which would allow Texas to be admitted by a simple majority vote in the two Houses, rather than requiring a two-thirds vote in the Senate. The House of Representatives endorsed annexation on January 25, 1845. Then on February 26, the Senate did the same. The resolution was signed by Tyler and sent to Texas. Texas needed only to accept statehood.

To the astonishment of many, however, President Jones did not immediately accept the resolution. Mexico, in the meantime, had slipped in with an alternate offer: recognition of Texan independence and a trade agreement of considerable value – but only if Texas did not join the United States. The simple truth was that

Mexico did not want the aggressive expansionism of the United States right across the Rio Grande. An independent Texas was highly preferable. While Texas had long wished for annexation to the United States, the idea of retaining their independence was appealing for some. However, Mexico had not instilled much in the way of confidence in their relations. It was the duty of President Jones to present both offers to the Texan Congress.

On July 4, 1845 (a day selected precisely for its importance), the Texan Congress met in Austin to vote on which offer to accept. The vote was overwhelmingly in favor of joining the United States. On December 29, 1845, U.S. President Polk signed the bill of formal admission. Texas government was to stay in effect until February. These were a rough couple of months for President Jones, who had to keep peaceful and polite relations between the United States, Mexico, and Texas while they waited for February 16, when the newly elected governor James Henderson would take control under the United States government. But on that day, the final Texan President gave a gracious speech as the two republics were joined, then drew down the Texas flag and raised the flag of the United States in its place.

Texas Moves On, and the Rangers Come Along

In the decade following the Texas Revolution, Texas became less a wild country of uncertain outcomes. They had declared their independence and followed through with resolve even after both the Mexican Army and the Comanche nation would have seen them fall. After Texas gained statehood, the following year, war with Mexico was officially declared. The Texas Rangers remained a critical law enforcement organization and a paramilitary power, namely protecting Texan settlers from Native and Mexican threats.

During the Reconstructionist Period after the Civil War, the Rangers organization was temporarily dissolved but reformed quickly after Texas regained its governmental authority. As time progressed, the Rangers' role evolved into valuable law enforcement officers. This much is obvious, but it is more than a simple fact that the Rangers are "valuable law enforcement." For that matter, the same could be said for the Texas Highway Patrol. It was not simply that the Texas Rangers organization endured, but that it suffered as a specialized group, members always a breed apart, and a league beyond their fellow enforcement agencies. The Rangers have apprehended fugitives, investigated murders and police corruption, and even were active in stopping the assassination of President William Taft.

In a state of 29 million people, Texas today has only about 160 active Rangers, an elite number of people who have what it takes to fill that unique role. The Texas Rangers statewide headquarters are based in the capital city of Austin.

The Tumlinson Brothers' Fates

When John Jackson Tumlinson, Sr. died on the Guadalupe River in 1823, his sons started on a path toward service to the protection of Texas, not as ordinary militiamen but as the specialized volunteers whose duty was to protect the fledging Texians. As we know, sons Thomas Carney Tumlinson and Andrew Tumlinson were killed early in their lives. John Jackson Sr.'s three remaining sons served the Texas military and were captains in the Texas Rangers.

John Jackson Tumlinson, Jr.

More than any of his brothers, John Jackson, Jr. was in the thick of the significant points in the Texas Revolution. Because of this, he has been the focal point of our history. His story seems best to encompass the emergence of the self-made heroes who were the early Texas Rangers.

From the time his father died, John Jackson Jr. protected the Texans from Native attacks and Mexican forces. When conflict ignited with Mexico, he was one of the first to volunteer and served twelve months as a Ranger. Still, he had ridden out with ranging companies even before the title of "Ranger" was adopted by the state as official and distinguished. He was the first man to organize a company of rangers under the authority of the Texas government.

Complete records of his service have been lost over time, but it is known that John Jackson Jr. continued to serve as a Ranger for several years following the conclusion of the Texas Revolution. Like his younger brothers Joseph and Peter, he often organized men to strike back at raiding Native parties. After Texas became part of the United States, there was hope that the United States military would take a more active role in these duties.

Still, their input was never sufficient to match the continuous protection of the Rangers.

John Jackson, Jr.'s life ended prematurely in 1853, a mere year before he would have been fifty years old. At the time, he was living in DeWitt County near his brothers Joseph and Peter. In his lifetime, John Jackson Jr. was married four times, but despite this seems to have only one heir who survived long enough to have her own family, his daughter Amanda, whom Peter Tumlinson raised in his own home after John Jackson Jr's. death, and who eventually married Cullen Edwards.

Joseph Tumlinson

Joseph Tumlinson, who at age 12 joined in on the raid to avenge the death of his father John Jackson Tumlinson, Sr., spent his life in the service of Texas – it was simply that this service was not always performed through strictly legal channels. In addition to his Texas army service during the Texas Revolution, he protected Texans against any Native threats in his region for twenty-five years. Accounts of his deeds tended to polarize him as either a hero or a menace – a viewpoint that did not change over the man's lifetime. He was known to be an accomplished gunfighter.

Joseph lost his first wife, Johanna, at some time during the Texas Revolution. In an interesting coincidence, his second wife became Elizabeth Newman, the daughter of Joseph Newman, the very man who had accompanied John Jackson Tumlinson, Sr. on his fatal trip.

Following the Texas revolution, Joseph Tumlinson spent decades of his life in adventures, some of which, while helpful, had questionable legality – but then again, legitimacy always came in a distant second to "necessity" in Texas's formative years. For example, Joseph formed his group of "regulators" to curb cattle rustling in his county. They were known to be judge, jury, and, yes, executioner, in the matters of captured rustlers, without consulting any outside law enforcement.

There is some reason to think the necessity for his behavior was legitimate, as Texas was on the losing side of the Civil War and subject to a great deal of confusion and abuse in the Reconstruction years that followed. Lawlessness was once again rampant throughout the state until finally, the dust cleared enough for an authentic Texan government to take charge. When law enforcement returned to the state, Joseph was commissioned to work for a state police company. As one might expect, power plays factored into the competition for which state police company would hold the most power and jurisdiction. As a result of this in-fighting, Joseph also played a part in the infamous Sutton-Taylor Feud, mostly because he was friendly to the Suttons' side in the fight.

In November of 1874, Joseph found religion; he was saved and baptized at a missionary meeting. In his *Genealogy*, Samuel Tumlinson relays that a local woman severely criticized the minister for not holding Joseph underwater long enough to drown him. Unfortunately, before having a chance to show he had changed his unruly ways, Joseph became ill and died. Perhaps righteous living did not agree with him. But in the man's eulogy, it was admitted that things would be less lively in Texas without him.

Peter Tumlinson

Peter was the Tumlinson son who had remained in Arkansas for a time before joining his family in Texas in approximately 1830. He fought in the cavalry during the Texas Revolution.

Peter Tumlinson joined the Rangers in 1835, and in 1859 he commanded his mounted volunteers, three of whom were his sons (Absolom, William, and Joseph), to quell the Cortina Disturbances.

In 1859, a stretch of the Rio Grande border was left unprotected when the U.S. military forces stationed there were temporarily called away. Juan N. Cortina, a local Mexican from a Texan family, began to cause trouble. Though his own family was of a specific respected class, Cortina took up what his class might call the "rabble" and was considerably influential among the discontented people. With his new cronies, he began to raid ranches close to the border. In September of that year, he raided Rio Grande City, looting the town and killing many of its citizens. He took control there, and his bands of raiders followed suit, taking towns all along the border between Texas and Mexico.

A Ranger Company led by Captain Peter Tumlinson (nicknamed "Old Uncle Pete" by his men) was the first organized Texan force to strike back at Cortina. He engaged Cortina and his men in several encounters; more Rangers arrived, and the U.S. military eventually returned to help, and they together drove Cortina out of Rio Grande City. Cortina continued making trouble, however, and as late as December of 1859, Old Uncle Pete, at the age of 57, led his Rangers on the front line of the fight against Cortina's organization. Mexicans were terrified of Peter Tumlinson, and Old Uncle Pete's methods caused consternation among the more organized military. But Old Uncle Pete (who was once criticized by the Texas Rangers for being armed only with his fists and chasing bandits into Mexican territory) felt that Rangers fought better with less discipline, and maybe he was right.

After defending the Rio Grande and Nueces River for almost two decades, Peter moved to Carrizo Springs with his wife, Harriet. There he died in 1876.

Texas Legends

As we know it today, the founding of Texas is a story of complication and reconciliation, of an incredible spirit of adventure and faultless bravery, of lies and promises broken, of integrity in the face of diversity, of astonishing crimes and admirable virtues. It is the story of some of the most challenging people alive, who persevered despite the stressors and dangers of the untamed country, despite the aggressions of a villainous dictator from Mexico City determined to break their wills. Nature that strong does not quickly leave a people, and it certainly must remain in the descendants of those original 300 who joined

Stephen Austin to create a new way of life in this place where few others were brave enough to try.

Tumlinson's descendants became as intertwined with Texas history as a family could be. Multiple descendants (both men and women) served in the military or Texas law enforcement, with sixteen known descendants serving as elite Texas Rangers.

The last known Tumlinson Ranger was Emanuel Avant "Dogie" Wright, who retired from service in 1951 to serve as sheriff of Hudspeth County. Dogie Wright descended directly from the marriage of Joseph Tumlinson and Elizabeth Newman. Dan Kilgore's book, *A Ranger Legacy*, is dedicated to the Dogie Wright, "last of the Tumlinson Rangers. A credit to his name and calling."

We believe the same can be said for all descendants of the long and proud Tumlinson line, which has always answered the call to protect the public so peace can prevail.

References:

Bell, Verner Lee. *From Whence We Came: John Jackson Tumlinson and Elizabeth Plemmons, Their Descendants and Connections.* 1999. Landmark Publishing.

blockhousecreek.org

Deem, James M. *Primary Source Accounts of the Mexican-American War.* 2006. Enslow Publishers.

Kilgore, D.E. *A Ranger Legacy: 150 Years of Service to Texas.* 1973. Madrone Press.

Lindley, Thomas Ricks. *Alamo Traces: New Evidence and New Conclusions.* Republic of Texas Press, 2003.

Moore, Stephen L. "Texas Rangers at the Battle of the Alamo." *Texas Ranger Dispatch Magazine.* www.texasranger.org

The Real West: The Texas Rangers. (1993) Directed by Craig Haffner.

Revolution & Republic. With Stephen L. Hardin, Ph.D. at www.diogeneslantern.com.

samuelamaverick.blogspot.com/2013/01/texas-homes.html

Smithwick, Noah. *The Evolution of a State* or *Recollections of Old Texas Days*. [c1900] Gammel Book Company, Austin, Texas.

Sonsofdewittcounty.org

Swanson, Doug J. *The Bold and Brutal History of the Texas Rangers*. 2020. Viking.

Handbook of Texas. Sponsored by the Texas State Historical Association. Tshaonline.org/handbook.

Tumlinson, Samuel H. *Tumlinson, a Genealogy*. Privately published and copyrighted by Samuel H. Tumlinson.

Webb, Walter Prescott. *The Texas Rangers: A Century of Frontier Defense*. 1965. The University of Texas Press.

Wilbarger, J.W. *Indian Depredations in Texas*. 1890. Texas State Library.

About Myself

Houston has been wonderful to me and taught me that you should never give up no matter how difficult the challenges. My life is an example of how our potential is limitless if we never give up. In my twenties, I was a Papa John's pizza delivery driver. Most of my free time was spent playing bass guitar, trying to sell insurance, and tinkering toward a college degree (that took my nine years to complete).

I dreamed big and never lost faith.

As a young man, while volunteering in a political campaign, I met former Texas Secretary of State Jack Morris Rains, who inspired me to become a lawyer. Having decided what I wanted to do, I attended the University of Phoenix and struggled with the LSAT.

Although my grades weren't ideal, I searched for law schools that possibly would accept me. Fortunate enough, a small establishment called Thomas M. Cooley Law School wanted me to attend. So I packed my bags and moved to a tiny apartment in Lansing, Michigan. I worked odd jobs, interned at Michigan Attorney General's Office, and graduated law school with a Cum Laude distinction.

Today, I own Dick Law Firm. We represent thousands of Texas consumers with their denied or underpaid property insurance claims. These are the types of claims where homeowners have damage to their roof due to a storm, and their insurance company wants to make any excuse for not paying for the damage. Insurance law is a field that is rather personal to me since my paternal grandmother (who became widowed due to WWII) was the first female insurance agent for American General. In that regard, I recognize the faith that consumers have in my firm to help them in their time of need.

As a lifetime learner, I was fortunate to start an MBA at Rice University during the Coronavirus pandemic. The academic work was good for my mind and spirit during those uncertain times. In itself, getting accepted to Rice was quite the feat since I had previously applied twice and been rejected.

Giving back to the public is crucial to me. In that respect, I served an unpaid elected position as a trustee for the Harris County Department of Education. Although I was the only Republican on the board, the six Democrats (each of which I consider a dear friend) wanted me to operate as their president of the board of trustees.

I believe this was because education is too important of an issue to be partisan. And, I have to admit, the work that we have accomplished has been spiritually gratifying. For instance, we've done some great stuff, like starting Texas's first public recovery high school, an initiative to increase child literacy, and a program to reimburse teachers for their expenses when buying school supplies. We did all of this while repeatedly lowering property taxes.

I'm happily married to Danielle, and we share two beautiful daughters, Grace and Caroline. And, of course, a proud descendent of the Tumlinson family. ♥

If you are interested in contacting Hon. Eric Dick, for speaking engagements or events, he can be reached –

- by telephone at (888) 660-0088 x 700,
- through email at eric@dicklawfirm.com, or
- by visiting his law firm's website at www.dicklawfirm.com.

Prayer

When I wrote this book, the last few years have been difficult for all of Texas. In Houston, many residents suffered from a horrible explosion that took lives and destroyed home. Immediately following, our world suffered from a once-in-a-lifetime pandemic that causes chaos, fear, and uncertainty in our lives. Finally, a winter storm freeze and rolling blackouts hit our state that devised many Texans to suffer from pipe bursts, property damages, death, and other distress. And, if it helps, no matter how hard our times are, please remember that our ancestor's experiences were much more draconian.

Nevertheless, despite our hardships, there is an opportunity to help others through kindness. Personal prayer is essential in light of the problems our world is facing. We trust God, strengthening our faith by devoting our time to cultivating empathy and understanding for others. We transition to love during difficult times. Amen to that.

No eye has seen,
no ear has heard,
and no mind has imagined
what God has prepared for
those who love him.
1 Corinthians 2:9

www.ingramcontent.com/pod-product-compliance
Lightning Source LLC
Chambersburg PA
CBHW072004090426
42740CB00011B/2078